Fly Fishing
In The Northwest
Territories of Canada

Chris Hanks

Frank
Amato

PORTLAND

Note To Readers

Many lodges and outfitters are mentioned in the text. I tried to use operations I knew had good reputations as examples. There are many other fine facilities that simply did not fit the text.

A more complete list can be obtained from the Government of the Northwest Territories by calling their toll free number at 1-800-661-0788 to request a current copy of *Canada's Northwest Territories Explorer's Guide*. The addresses and phone numbers of all the lodges I have mentioned can be found in this useful source document. When planning a trip north, talk with a variety of operators and find one that will tailor a trip to your needs.

Dedicated to:

George Pellissey—my friend and travelling partner.

About the Cover:

Wally Allen on Snowbird Lake, Kazan River. Photo by John Gierach..

All inquiries should be addressed to:

Frank Amato Publications, Inc.
P.O. Box 82112, Portland, Oregon 97282

Book Design and Layout: Alan Reid
Photos: Chris Hanks unless otherwise noted

Printed in Canada
1 3 5 7 9 10 8 6 4 2

ISBN Softbound:
1-57188-080-1

Acknowledgments

I would like to thank, George Pellissey, Tony Tatti, Paul Wright, Gabe Etchinelle, John Tetso, George Barnaby, John Shae, Dale Freschi, Tom Andrews, Frank Drygeese, Greg Cook, Ray Bradshaw, Mary McCreadie, and the many others who spent time on the water with me in the NWT over the years.

Ellen Pollard of Brabant Lodge and Ragnar Wesstrom of Enodah Wilderness Travel provided me with spectacular fly fishing opportunities.

Chummy Plummer of Plummer's Arctic Fishing Lodges, John Pollard of Brabant Lodge, Judith Wright of Drum Lake Lodge, Keith Sharp of Ferguson Lake Lodge, Gary Gurke of Nueltin fly-in Lodges, Tom Faess of Great Canadian Ecoventures, Alex Hall of Canoe Arctic Inc., Wally Schaber of Black Feather Wilderness Adventures, Morris Modest and Walter Baya from Deline, Clayton Burke of the Taiga Tour Company, Bern Will Brown of Colville Lake Lodge, Gary Jaaeb of True North Safaris, Barb Dillion of Tourism, Marketing and Develo-pment— Government of the North-west Territories, Ron Tologanak of the Kugluktuk Angoniatit Association, Gordon Hamre and Bob Gamble from Parks Canada, Laurie Pelly from the Lands Department of Nunavut Tunngavik Inc., Warren Wright from North- Wright Air, North Douglas from Edzo, NWT, and Gordon Lennie from Yellowknife, have all provided information for this book.

John Gierach, Aaron Herter, Mary McCreadie, David Pelly, Gary Jaaeb, Chummy Plummer and George Low contributed photographs.

Gary Almidia from the Anglers Covey in Colorado Springs, tied the flies for the book. He did a wonderful job working from my home-brewed recipes.

George Low and James Reist of the Canadian Department of Fisheries and Oceans provided me with technical assistance. All interpretation of that information is responsibility of the author.

Nancy Hanks, Clay Roberts and Cooper Longford read the manuscript. I wish to thank them for their many helpful comments.

My skeptical friend Jim Raffan who wishes to go to his grave believing I have never caught a fish on a fly rod. Believe me Jimmy, it ain't so.

A choice Arctic grayling from the Lockhart River near MacKay Lake.

Craig Cook on the North Arm of Great Slave Lake.

Table Of Contents

Preface

Fly Fishing in the Northwest Territories was written for those drawn to the Canadian waters that flow into the Arctic Ocean. Based largely on my own experiences, I hope you find my angler's journey across the north a pleasure.

Writing this book has not been without its controversies. There are those fishermen who having discovered the splendor of the north, feel the only way to protect the unspoiled wonder of the Arctic and subarctic is to hide it from others. Some northerners feel that anyone who comes from outside should go to a lodge. They are contrasted by the "free spirits" who explore the north with a canoe and a fishing rod. I believe that in the end, the only way to protect the rivers and lakes of the north is to educate the populace, so they understand that Arctic waters are a treasure to be carefully used, and ardently protected. A sense of stewardship must be developed if northern drainages are to be preserved for the next generation. Advocating the preservation of the free running Arctic rivers requires informed users. There is a fine balance between the consumptive values that require more electric power generation, oil recovery, and mining against the need for unblemished places.

The Northwest Territories is not an unknown wilderness. It has been lived in for thousands of years by Native Dene and Inuit who call the land home. It has been combed by fur traders, hunters, and fishermen for profit and sport. Geologists and miners continue to extract its wealth from the ground while hydrologists eye the untapped potential of its rivers to supply power to hungry cities. Bluntly, in the language of land planners, the Northwest Territories land use policy is one of multiple use. None of this is meant to detract from the fact that the Territories is still a wonderfully wild, quiet, sometimes lonely place to escape the pressures of modern life. The message is clear, however, that fishermen must be aware of the "values at risk" and be active in the fight to protect the cold clear waters of the

Caribou along the Lockhart River.

On the Beach at Snowbird Lake Lodge.

Arctic. Miraculously, one of the best ways to help this fight is to go north and fish your way into memories, so you will never forget why you love wild rivers and lonely lakes.

Fly Fishing in the Northwest Territories is not just about fishing. The essays are designed to set the mood for a northern trip. They will help you select an option that fits your abilities and schedule. The essays are broken down by geographic regions—the Mackenzie Mountains, Mackenzie Lowlands, Canadian Shield and the Barren Lands. I have not attempted an all inclusive guide, but rather have drawn freely from my personal experiences, in the belief they will entertain and pique your interest.

This publication is intended only as an introduction. Northern river and lake conditions are highly variable; water levels are capable of change from day to day and year to year. The ownership of northern lodges changes over time. If you are considering planning your own wilderness trip, this volume does not replace the need for accurate canoeing trip reports, detailed maps, scouting rapids, and appropriate judgment and skills. Neither the author or the publisher can accept any responsibility for misinterpretation of information or the failure of fishermen to accurately assess their own situation.

Since leaving the Northwest Territories in the fall of 1991, the places I came to know in the 10 years I lived in the NWT, continue to provide recurrent images. How can one forget caribou and Dall's sheep on steep mountain slopes above the Keele River, Arctic grayling in the boiling water below the middle Cascade on the Kazan River, or a Lynx swimming the Yellowknife River one spectacular fall day, when the aspens have turned translucent yellow. Ultimately the pull of that distant land was too strong, as I close this manuscript we are packing to move back to Yellowknife.

Chris Hanks
Victor, Colorado - December 1995

Introduction
Fly Fishing In The Northwest Territories

Long before I ventured into the Northwest Territories, boyhood notions of Arctic charr and Arctic grayling in cold northern rivers, created an imagined context for the rainbow trout I stalked in western New York. My youthful perceptions of the Arctic were a complex jumble of half thoughts about the tree line, endless herds of caribou, polar bears and Natives who still lived by hunting and fishing. All of these perceptions hedge at the truth, but the reality is far more varied in a land that stretches from the Mackenzie Mountains of the northern Rockies, to the Arctic Islands that reach toward the pole. During the decade I wandered the Northwest Territories, I began to learn the ways of a land with seemingly endless water. Exploring a headwaters stream in the Mackenzie Mountains, drifting in a canoe along a tree lined lake on the Canadian Shield, and paddling the broad swift flows of the Barren Land rivers, the affinity between fly fishing and wilderness canoe travel was obvious. The land surpasses my youthful expectations.

The years are a blur of discoveries associated with learning the waters of the Arctic drainage. Often skunked, but seldom hungry, the northern rivers slowly gave up their secrets. When I close my eyes there are scenes of the Keele River, Great Bear Lake and the Kazan River that will always return. These memories blend with thoughts of future trips and become plans.

Coming north is more than a canoe trip or fishing junket. It is a step away from instant electronic communications, and a chance for dangling conversation around the campfire. The thrill of a lake trout stripping the line from your reel is accentuated by the scene around you. Images of that fish will be forever mixed with the smell of spruce, the golden eagle that soared over your head, and the sound of the paddle.

Deciding to fly fish in the Northwest Territories is a decision to try something different. For those brought up on browns, rainbow, brookies, and cutthroats you must get your mind around some different species. Oh— there are a few stocked rainbows in lakes near Yellowknife, and Hay River in the western part of the Territories, but they are not the stock and trade of fishing in the north. Fly fishing in the NWT is built around Arctic charr, Arctic grayling, lake trout, Dolly Varden, bull trout, northern pike, walleyed pike and lake whitefish. Before you curl your lip at grayling and whitefish give them a fair chance. Veteran fly fisherman and writer, the late Roderick Haig-Brown, once said of Arctic grayling that "... trout could learn a good deal from them about surface feeding and honest response to a well-presented artificial". The grayling has left me with many of my finest memories and shapes my perception of good dry fly fishing. Until you have experienced the fight of a four-pound lake whitefish on your line, don't judge them harshly. Lake trout are the object of trollers in many parts of North America. Cold water temperatures throughout the summer in the Territories, however, give you a better than average opportunity at trophy size fish on streamers such as a Jack Sprat, large caddis nymphs, scuds, and dry flies. The deep hard fight of the lakers is an experience long remembered. The lure of big northern pike attracts fly fishermen north, who are looking for new thrills with streamers. Unless you are lucky enough to angle some of the isolated drainages of the Mackenzie Mountains, you will not run into bull trout. When you do, however, they provide a wonderful juxtaposition to the Arctic grayling found in the same waters. Northern bulls fight deep and hard in splendid contrast to the acrobatics of the grayling. Alternating between the two species adds sparkle to the long hours of Arctic twilight. Arctic charr draw many anglers north. The charr compares favourably with steelhead and salmon as a great fly rod fish. Though poorly documented, rumours persist that brook trout have spread into a few Keewatin rivers from Hudson's Bay, and a mysterious run of chum salmon ascends the Mackenzie and Slave rivers 1,500 miles, to the Rapids of the Drowned on the NWT/Alberta border.

When one thinks of fly fishing in Canada's far north, it is hard not to assume an ideal situation where world's records lurk in the offing. The fish stocks of the north are, however, extremely fragile. The same cold water that makes great fly rod action on lake trout also make for extremely slow growth rates. Fish in the NWT often take several extra years to reach sexual maturity. Growth rates are extremely slow due to water temperatures that are below optimum body temperature levels for metabolism in fish. The short Arctic and subarctic summers are simply not long enough to grow fish quickly. Great Bear Lake for instance, is not ice free until the middle of July and is usually refrozen by late November. Practically speaking, the ice remains until long after the endless days of June that give life in the north its kick start in the race against winter. The long period of snow covered ice enclosure makes oxygen deprivation a threat for fish populations in many lakes. These factors make the population equilibrium delicate enough that thoughtless sport fishing can have a major impact on fish stocks. Over the last 25 years, selectively fishing schools of older larger grayling for trophy fish has resulted in a decrease in the average size of Arctic grayling around the outlet of Great Slave Lake. This led to fork limits being established in the mid-1970s, and restrictions on fishing during spawning on at least one creek. The Kakisa River spawning run is now only a catch and release fishery. Great Bear Lake, the sixth largest fresh water lake in the world, has been impacted by sport angling pressure over the last 30 years. Maintaining Great Bear Lake as a premiere trophy fishery now requires reduced creel limits and a real effort by fishers to practice catch and release. This means a switch in gear for many people. Large fish caught by deep trolling and brought to the surface too quickly can not generally be successfully released because the fish will suffer from the bends. Light spinning and fly tackle with barbless hooks used in shallow water, is slowly becoming the new order of the day for Great Bear Lake. In 1990, for the first time, it was necessary to close the world famous Tree River Arctic charr fishery in late August once the waters 700 fish quota had been reached. Sport fishing during Arctic grayling spawning runs remains a challenge to fisheries managers. The impact of industrial pollution from acid mine tailings is a time bomb slowly ticking in a few NWT drainage systems. It is only a matter of time before an abandoned tailings pond leaks. The development of forestry operations and hydro-electric projects are spectres that loom on the horizon in some areas of the Territories. Combine these threats with airborne toxins from the industrial world now found in Arctic waters and it is evident that while the northern cold water fishery is still very healthy, it faces an uncertain future. Action by responsible individuals and government is necessary to preserve the fabulous wilderness experience available today.

For most people the right outfitter is the best way of translating your vision into a northern angling reality. You must, however, ask the right questions beforehand, as fly fishermen are not the primary clients of northern lodges, which cater to boat based trolling and spin casting. If you want to stream or river fish it is important to ask what opportunities a lodge offers before you book your reservation. Once you have arrived make sure the management remembers you want a guide who will work the rivers or knows lake locations where you will be successful. The north is a big place, consequently tapping the right local knowledge is key to your success. Familiarity with northern waters is gained only by experience. It is a quality many claim and few possess. Do your homework, ask the right questions, have reasonable expectations and you will be on your way to a good experience. Seek good fishing,

but do not set your heart on a world record.

Having a good guide is important for more reasons than "going after the big one". The solitude and unblemished water that led you to the Arctic have their price. You are a long way from the myriad of rescue and medical facilities we are accustomed to in modern urban society. On the barrens your travelling party is your support and social network. Your experience will not be enhanced by presumption, posturing and "proving yourself". Northern rivers typically have larger water volumes than many fly fishers are used to wading. Couple this with low air and water temperatures and it means that a trip "through the rapids", can be serious trouble. Drowning is only the first danger. Once you get out of the water, unless you are properly cared for, hypothermia can still kill you. Respecting your guide's opinion about safe wading is essential, even if you think he is being too conservative. Remember he may have to risk his life to save you. If an incident does hap-

Canoe on the Lockhart River.

Photo by Gary Jaeb

pen, your guide's actions in those first critical minutes are essential to your safety. John Gierach's amusing tale of having his guide motor-up and quietly tell him to "Get in zee boat!" moments before his waders filled in a rapids on the Kazan River, is a classic example of an incident that ended happily.

Despite all the qualifiers about expectations, sometimes simply "coming north" and putting yourself in the hands of a guide can turn your dreams into angling reality. During a refuelling stop for our Single Otter aircraft at Bronsons' Lodge, on the east end of Great Bear Lake, in 1990, one of the guides quietly let it slip that fly rod tippet records for Arctic grayling and lake trout had recently been broken by a lodge guest. Apparently, the gentleman who broke the trout record had gone to Great Bear Lake intent on setting a new standard. He arrived in camp on Saturday. Tuesday morning he landed his record. The north is a place where fishing dreams can come true. Lodges across the Territories, with their hard won local knowledge, make a "successful" catch possible for those who choose that route.

There is another way, however, for those who seek the less travelled flow. Planning and undertaking your own trip, however, takes advanced wilderness skills. Once you leave the fold of established outfitters and guides you are on your own. If you have the know how and are willing to build on your experience with each trip, there are incredible waters to be explored. A canoe and backpack set you free.

Finding a spring creek high in the Mackenzie Mountains full of two-pound grayling is an experience not easily forgotten. The discovery is sweeter yet when you can smile non-committally at the local outfitter when he asks where you got the fish, knowing they came from a spruce bound creek virtually in his own backyard. On other days there are lakes full of scuds, with no fish, that leave you swearing. After all when a beautiful piece of water has no fish, there must be reason, right?

Roderick Haig-Brown maintained that fishers in some subtle way are all "...hoping to create or recreate some ideal situation". Steeped in the literature of our sport, I muse about brook trout in the Nipegon River before the hydro-electric dams, and recall stories of them in the meadow streams of my native upstate New York. I knew large wild speckles briefly in northern Quebec before the Caniapiscau River was flooded by Hydro-Quebec. Wild salmonidae of a different sort still grace the untamed rivers of the Northwest Territories. Big fish are a reality here but not a roadside panacea. The search for that piece of water that is seldom trod, where a low quiet stalk will lead to a steadily rising six-pound Arctic grayling still preoccupies me. Grayling are the archetype of a fish that requires cold clear water. Their retreat and extinction in Michigan and diminished range in Montana make them all the more precious in their remaining Arctic strong holds. In the NWT, their continued numbers speak well of good water quality, intact forests and minimal impact by man. Yet even here, their frequent willingness to take artificials makes them susceptible to over fishing. Their tendency to school by age means that once a pod of large fish are located an entire year class of spawning adults can be carelessly removed from the breeding cycle. Arctic grayling populations that receive even modest fishing pressure need to be part of a managed catch and release programme.

The Arctic grayling has delighted me through countless long northern evenings, as the moment of twilight typical of southerly latitudes, is spread over hours. They have honed my dry fly skills as I have sought to drift flies over rising fish from every conceivable angle, and they taught me the mystical art of upstream nymphing without a strike indicator. Learning this latter trick lead to bad Zen jokes about "Kung fu" fishing by my archaeological crew one summer. "Oh grasshopper, there is a fish on your line. Master, how do you know of this unlikely event? Grasshopper, you must sense that the fish is waiting for you to strike..." Searching brooks and ponds across the Mackenzie Mountains, I have found grayling in the oddest spots. Half-pound fish in the pools of Doh Doh Creek's saline waters or tucked away deep in the blackened undercuts of Echo Canyon leave one questioning traditional wisdom. Echo Creek drops 200 feet into a canyon so narrow that the tops of the walls virtually meet, allowing only the merest sliver of light to enter the graylings' lair.

My search for grayling on light tackle lead to a large trout in a huge eddy, breaking a new nine-foot, 5/6, four-piece rod, on the Kazan River several summers ago. The ensuing frantic radio messages to my wife to put another rod on our only resupply flight, drew chuckles from those who succeeded in getting my trusty old 8 weight on the plane. Having learned the hard way, I now carry at least a pair of pack rods—my replacement 5/6 and a stouter nine-1/2-foot, 7/8

for big water. When weight allows I now also tuck in a nine foot, 4/5, four piece so I can indulge in smaller flies and lighter tippets when wind and water permit. Weight and space often severely limit the equipment one can carry, but I have learned never to begrudge the space needed for a spare rod and an extra spool of line.

At the risk of neglecting the other species, I have prattled on about the Arctic grayling, because for me, this colourful little fighter typifies angling in the Northwest Territories. It is in the best of the undisturbed waters from the high mountains to the Arctic coast. Often it lightens a hard day as it leaps with abandon. Finally, the lure of the elusive six-pound Arctic grayling demands a continued search of the seldom paddled byways.

Guided or on your own, fly fishing in the Territories will change your view of angling. You will remember big water you could not wade, whose eddies yielded only a few of their secrets. Little known spring creeks which bubble from mountainsides, spotted with the rhythm of summers hatches, will become your measure of a good stream. Some days knowing they exist is enough, at other times, however, you long to return and cast on those distant waters.

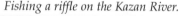

Fishing a riffle on the Kazan River.

Photo by John Gierach

Chapter One

To see further than you can walk in a day

Fly fishing on the Canadian Barren Lands is a pleasure unknown to most anglers. It is an experience so rare, that one must think about it for months in advance. To spend a summer on one of the great Barren Land rivers—the Kazan, Thelon, Back, Dubawnt or Coppermine is an adventure from a time when journeys still took months or years. Fishing is part of life on the trail. By the end of the trip photographs of three-pound grayling, lake trout chowder, and flies dubbed with musk ox quiviout (wool) plucked from willow thickets, have become part of the experience.

Herds of caribou flowing across the landscape dissolve days. A photographer stalking the shaggy visage of a musk ox silhouetted against the horizon, may be distracted by a peregrine falcon's nest tucked high on a craggy face. Watching Arctic wolf cubs playing on a glacial esker, or the appearance of a solitary Barren Land grizzly on a hillside, will often stretch a quick lunch break far into the afternoon. It is a land where time is measured against the onset of winter, and geologic movement. The events of the day set the course of the day.

Fishing on the barrens is a given, taken for granted by many Barren Land travellers as part of the ambiance and a way to augment their food supply. It is more, of course, for while your camera allows you to record the landscape, and the canoe lets you ply the surface of the river, your fly swirling down into an eddy provides a glimpse of the lower reaches of the river. It completes the trilogy of air, land, and water that dominates days on the barrens.

The contrast between life on the land and existence hundreds of miles to the south, is accentuated by the solitude of the great northern silence. The early morning pterodactyl cries of mating sand hill cranes, a rising wind rustling in the willows at noon, and the roar of the rapids at night are the only sound that intrude on the day. Conversations with companions seem hushed as the land simply absorbs the sound.

Bob Gamble, at Parks Canada in Yellowknife, and I often mused about the splendor of the tree line near Lynx Lake, with the promise of the brawling upper Thelon River and the undulating Barren Lands beyond. Standing at the edge of the trees on the shore of Lynx Lake, looking out onto the barrens has left an image in my mind like a fine photograph. It is a powerful landscape full of contrasts, that was at its most beguiling that fall day with the red tinge of autumn on the tundra.

A lot of canoeing fishermen consider travelling on the barrens the archetype of Arctic canoe trips. The scale of a trip on the barrens, however, makes planning your own "expedition" a more formidable task than descending one of the mountains or boreal forest rivers. The flight out from Yellowknife, Fort Smith, Norman Wells, or Inuvik is longer and more expensive. One needs to carefully consider how to retrieve canoes from an isolated river mouth or a community with limited air service. Getting people out is easy but canoes can be an expensive problem. With the exception of the Hanbury/Thelon and Kazan which flow into Baker Lake, near the Inuit community of Baker Lake, the Barren Land rivers drain directly into the Arctic Ocean. The mouths of the Horton and Back rivers mark the beginning of a treacherous sea voyage or a very expensive aircraft charters. Conveniently, the Coppermine River ends in a community with barge service. If the trip is timed correctly, the canoes can be thrown on a barge for Hay River and the people can jump on a scheduled flight for Yellowknife.

When a trip longer than four weeks is planned, the problem of carrying enough food without scheduling a re-supply flight, takes very careful consideration. I have toughed it out on commercially available freeze-dried food, pasta and beans many times, but you can get a more varied and better diet if you prepare your own. Home drying food will require a lot of planning and preparation time. One time, Jack Grieves and I canoed the Hayes River in northern Manitoba on a big bag of potatoes, onions, and carrots supplemented by all the fish we could catch. I would recommend a lot more preparation so that you are not reduced to that extreme. Once a menu has been selected, it may take a couple of months to get food prepared, meals tested and everything packed. It is important to be honest with yourself. If a re-supply flight is needed to complete the trip then it is best to plan on the expense and have a Cessna 185 come out and meet you. It may sound romantic, but it is no longer acceptable for canoeists to carry a gun and try and live off the land.

On the barrens you will need a 17-1/2-foot AVS or Kevlar prospector canoe. On a shorter mountain or boreal forest trip, a two boat party is reasonable, but given the distances involved on a Barren Land trip, three boats are really necessary both for safety and to carry an adequate food supply. It would be nice to be able to use 18-foot boats, but unfortunately you can only get one 18-foot canoe in a Twin Otter. Three 17-1/2-foot, high volume canoes that will sandwich together inside a Twin Otter and still leave room for packs and people are a must. Depending on the trip, you will probably still need a second smaller load into the riverhead to accommodate your starting weight.

A three boat party raises the question of who the other five people who go along should be. A seven week trip requires a group that will be comfortable with each other through thick or thin for a whole summer. Canoeing partners, like fishing buddies, tend to grow out of trips over the years.

I remember the first time I was on the Arctic coast south of the Hall Beach DEW line station on the Melville Peninsula. I was overwhelmed by being able to see further than I could walk in three days. The open vistas of the barrens are wonderful, but I also find the vastness to be disconcerting at times. The contrast in July between the blossoms of the Arctic lupines and poppies tucked among the rocks and the vast horizons is truly awesome. Because firewood is often in such short supply, you cannot sit around a roaring fire after a cold wet day of paddling. A roaring gas stove does not replace the romance or warmth of a wood fire. I remember how frustrated I was on the Kazan River, after one of

Photo by Mary McCreadie

Jess Tate with a Kazan River Lake Trout.

the boats dumped, as we waited for several hours while companions warmed up in our sleeping bags. A roaring fire would have made a tremendous difference not only as a heat source but also to keep everyone's spirits up. The Chipewyan and Dogribs used to carry wood out on the barrens with them when they went to hunt. The last grove of trees before the barrens was important for Native hunters after caribou and remains so for the modern canoeist.

If you decide on a Barren Land trip, try and select a route that intercepts one of the caribou herds—Bathurst, Beverly, Kaminuriak, or Bluenose on their way from the calving grounds. What would a trek to the tundra be without sitting in the midst of thousands of animals flowing by your camp. There are always surprised looks when people see the "bathtub" ring of caribou hair along the banks of a river after a caribou herd crosses. In the past, the coming of the caribou was the difference between life and death for the Inuit and Dene. When English adventurer John Hornby stayed on in what became the Thelon Game Sanctuary, after the caribou moved south into the forest for the winter, his entire party perished. That scarcity seems impossible on a bright summer's day when caribou seem to block the horizon line.

To follow and fish the Kazan, Thelon, Back, Mara, Burnside, Hood, Coppermine, Horton or Anderson rivers from the headwaters to the sea requires seven or eight weeks. Unfortunately, few of us can arrange our schedules to be away for that long.

Year by year there are more ways to go fishing on the Barren Lands as canoe guiding services, and more lodges, provide greater access to the lakes and rivers within reasonable time frames. My independent streak and canoeist bias is obvious, but not everyone is able to plan their own Barren Land expedition. If canoeing or rafting strikes your fancy, Tom Faess of Great Canadian Ecoventures does fishing and naturalist tours on the famous Thelon and Kazan rivers. On request, he will also run raft trips to accommodate drift fishermen through the Arctic grayling infested waters of the upper Thelon River. The float down from Whitefish Lake will offer the chance to drift 60 miles of white water that few people ever get the opportunity to fish. The rapids and canyon on the upper Thelon River

near the junction of the Hanbury River, make it less popular as a canoe route than the Hanbury/Thelon trip, but it is ideal as a raft trip. Around Labour Day, when the lake trout begin to run out of Whitefish Lake, it is hard to find better fly fishing.

Gary and Lois Gurke's Nueltin Lake fly-in Lodges straddle both the Manitoba/NWT border and the tree line. Treeline Lodge is located at the southern end of the lake. Nueltin Narrows is near the mid-point and Windy River is situated at the north end. Spring takes about three weeks to ascend the 120-mile length of Nueltin Lake. Anglers can move north with the receding ice edge, allowing them to experience the superb fishing that occurs when the trout are released from winter's grip. Water at the north end remains cold enough, that big lake trout at Seal Hole Rapids stay near the surface within reach of flies all summer. Fly fishermen on Nueltin Lake take lake trout, northern pike, and Arctic grayling. If they wish, guests can fly-out to fish for walleye on Keewatinkinokumaw Lake.

Keith Sharp's Ferguson Lake Lodge provides heli-fishing for lake trout and Arctic grayling out of their camp on Ferguson Lake. They have outpost camps at Yathkyed Lake on the Kazan River and on Kaminuriak Lake along the Maguse River. Fishing on Yathkyed Lake was a high point in my angling career. There was superb dry fly action for Arctic grayling in mid-July.

Doug Hill's Kasba Lake Lodge is located near the headwaters of the Kazan River in the transitional forests south of the tree line. It provides lake trout, Arctic grayling, and northern pike. One of the current fly rod tippet class records came out of the Kazan

Photo by John Gierach

Wally Allen with a Kazan River Arctic grayling.

River between Snowbird and Kasba lakes.

From July through August, Plummer's Lodge, Tree River Camp provides access to premier Arctic charr fishing on the Tree River. During late August and September, when the Arctic Charr come into the Coppermine River, guides from the Kugluktuk Angoniatit Association (i.e., the Coppermine Hunters and Trappers Association) take sports upriver to Bloody Falls to fish for charr.

While this is not a complete list, I have tried to provide a sampling of the outfitters and lodges that operate on the Barren Lands. It is not an endorsement of any particular operation but rather an attempt to give the angler some place to start their search.

Chapter Two

Prince River—Charr or were they grayling?

A crackling message over the trappers radio frequency, "...the Arctic charr are running at Prince River," sent us paddling across Baker Lake, in search of fresh fish from the sea. To northern fishermen, the mention of Arctic charr rings with a resonance not unlike the mention of steelhead and salmon. They are fish that spark passionate pursuit.

Unlike the high-volume Kazan River that requires fly fisherman to adapt their angling style, the Prince is a small river with a structure familiar to anyone who has fished a large free stone stream. It appears diminutive in relation to the vast rolling hills of treeless tundra that surround it. Yet all of the water cannot be covered from one bank. You cannot consistently cast across the flow. And when you pull up your hip boots to wade in and cover a pocket beyond your reach, you will discover it is not a shallow stream.

Arctic charr run into the small rivers and streams along the ragged north shore of Baker Lake. Rivers along the sandier, relatively shallow south shore do not have Arctic charr runs. Charr fishing along the famous Thelon River, which enters Baker Lake west of the community, is good upstream near Schultz Lake. The water around the river mouth is difficult. The Prince River is the best known of Baker Lake's north shore Arctic charr water.

Rising out of Whitehills Lake, 33 miles north of the community of Baker Lake, the mouth of the Prince River is only a short boat ride from town. It is reasonably accessible water, that would nicely compliment a lake trout and Arctic grayling trip to the lower Kazan River.

The level of the Prince River dramatically fluctuates throughout the short period of open water. During spring runoff in late June, you can canoe the length. By early August the Prince River is full of "rock gardens" which form lovely sections of pocket water between the deeper pools and swift runs. The lower water levels of fall frustrate canoeists but they are perfect for the fly fisherman in search of Arctic charr.

While paddling past Nunagiak Point on one of the Little Islands in Baker Lake, Jess Tate asked an Inuk who was slowly trolling by us, "How do you catch a charr?" He grinned and yelled back, "With a fly rod and a blue fly." I patted my rod case and smiled.

Land, at the mouth of the Prince River, came none too soon. We had been paddling across open water most of the day. With the exception of a brief break on the Little Islands, I had been folded up in the stern the entire time. My feet were not entirely certain they belonged to the rest of my body when I stepped out. Though August is marked by unstable weather on the Barren Lands, the afternoon winds had been mild and our crossing easy.

I climbed a hill to scout the fishing upstream. From there the Prince River was a winding ribbon of rapids. The dark blue runs and flashing white water contrasted sharply with the sedge tundra that stretches from its banks as far as the eye can see. Ultimately, the alternative between working the bay with a sinking tip line from a canoe or walking along the river trying to coax a rise left no choice. On stiff legs, I headed for the pocket water upstream.

Crouched against a granite outcrop, I cursed the mixed bag of tackle I had been left with after a long summer on the Barrens, casting a 6 weight line on an 8 weight rod. The combination was fine with a long line, but in the tight quarters below the final chute on the Prince River, I longed for a balanced outfit. With more luck than skill, I rolled a size 14 rusty-yellow Woolly Bugger onto the edge of the broken water; it flicked off a small standing wave and tucked under the froth. A moment later, the line tightened and a small Arctic charr exploded into the air. With steady pressure the eight-inch fish came quickly to heal. I slipped the hook and let it resume its journey.

Lacking waders, I worked along the west bank, fishing pockets and eddies. Several times, it would have been nice to have waded out to avoid conflicting currents. With careful reading of the water, however, it was possible to fish a lot of prime cover. A downstream presentation was easy. Working a fly from upstream demanded more care. Without vegetation to cover my advance to casting positions, there was a lot of plodding along on hands and knees. Soft moss to flop down on made up for some of the duck walking along the treeless banks. It was alpine meadow fishing on a grand scale.

The tundra grasses had turned brown. Dwarf willows were tinged with yellow and red. I missed the earlier brilliance of the Barrens in bloom but every season has its enchantments. On a hill off in the distance, I could make out a lone Inuk with a rifle watching for caribou. The fall caribou hunt starts when the days become cool enough that meat will not spoil when temporarily stored in rock cairns. Later, it is transported back to town with small ATVs or snowmobiles. A summer of grazing and the lower temperatures of autumn causes the animals to fatten and start their winter coats. Gone are the scruffy, warble fly infested beasts of a month ago. The skins were becoming prime for winter parkas. It was time for the Inuit of Baker Lake, to start putting up their winter supply of skins, meat and fat. If I am lucky, I will pick up some fresh caribou hair in town to tie flies with next winter.

Looking back into the edge of an eddy, I could see a nice grayling hanging below a rock. Rooting through a depleted fly box, I found one last Partridge and Orange to tie on. Carefully casting across the eddy, I dropped the fly on the tongue of current that rolled around the boulder. It bobbled along in the froth for a moment and then disappeared down a small keeper. The leader hesitated and I set the hook. With the fish running into the eddy toward me, I leapt up to keep tension on. Distracted by the gyrating line, an ankle grabbing willow nearly sent me into the river. I saved my pride and the fish on the line, with an improvisational dance step.

Upstream a few minutes later, another grayling broke loose when the point snapped off the hook. I retired the Partridge and Orange into a compartment of noble but disabled flies that each have stories to tell of a summer on the Barrens.

Switching to a February Red Stonefly, I continued upstream. Over the next six hours, the results were consistently successful. When hunger gnawed at my concentration, I began the 3-1/2-mile walk back to camp. It had been a satisfying day. I had taken and released two small Arctic charr on their way out to sea and a score of Arctic grayling. They were not big fish stories, but a crisp fall day along a delightful tundra river is hard to beat.

Later, in the community of Baker Lake, I tried to find out more about the run. Big Arctic charr had been in the bay off the Prince River, but so far they had only been gathered by Inuit with gill nets. If I had had another week then maybe, just maybe, I would have hit the sea run fish. Baker Lake in late August. My calendar is marked.

Prince River.

Photo by Mary McCreadie

Chapter Three

Kazan River—Fishing the Big Eddies

When I was assigned to coordinate scientific projects on a canoe survey along the Kazan River, I am shamed to admit my first thought was of Arctic grayling. The Kazan River was, after all, where Wally Allen had set a fly rod record for grayling a few years earlier. What more did I need to know? While reality forced me to minutely plan the archaeological, and pale-environmental projects, the aquatic world of the Arctic grayling set a tone that ran throughout the trip.

Archaeology is the perfect cover for a marauding fly fisherman. The camps of the Native Canadians who came before us, mark the caribou crossings and fisheries of the Kazan River. Years before, a Quebec-Hydro biologist working on the Caniapiscau River, in northern Quebec, had impressed on me the utility of the fly rod as a biological sampling device. Could there be a more perfect way to demonstrate the importance of fishing to generations of Caribou Inuit hunters on the barrens, than to ply the water before their ancient homes with fur and feathers?

As the moment of departure approached, I found I had been awake for hours staring out the window of the train as it rolled north out of the trees, across the open tundra toward Churchill, Manitoba. I mused that the Hudson's Bay Railroad is rumoured to be the only line in the world that runs up hill in both directions. Critics maintain the track sags into the muskeg bogs under the weight of a train, leaving the engine to pull its charge perpetually up a grade.

I wished I could find some coffee, but the dining car did not open until six a.m. When I finally got some breakfast, I savoured the greasy bacon and fresh eggs knowing they would be the last I would have before I reached Baker Lake in mid-August. My consumption of coffee was more restrained than I would have liked, but the thought of two hours on a cramped plane with no rest room tempered my behaviour.

Despite the ice a short distance away in Hudson's Bay, it was a beautiful warm late June morning when we rolled into town. Canoes were quickly unloaded from the baggage car of the Polar Bear Express and lashed to a borrowed pickup. After the first pot hole, it was obvious that the truck had no springs. I anchored myself between a canoe and a food pack and hung on as we lumbered across town to the float plane base. Ptarmigan Air's yellow Twin Otter rode gently beside the dock as we sandwiched three boats through the cargo door, piled in packs, and wedged six paddlers in seats along the port side. The plane slipped out into the lake, turned into the wind, and roared north toward the Barren Lands.

Skimming across polar bears in the dump, beluga whales in the Churchill River and past the ruins of Fort Prince of Wales, we reached our cruising altitude of 1,500 feet as we turned northwest along the tree line. I settled down for a circuitous trip to our base camp on Angikuni Lake. Along the way, we passed Nueltin Lake, scene of novelist Farley Mowat's famous books People of the Deer and Never Cry Wolf. On the approach to Ennadai Lake, we flew over the lonely remains of a government weather station and a Caribou Inuit village where starvation had stalked people in the late 1940s. Life on the barrens used to mean total dependence upon fish and caribou. When they failed, hunger followed. There is so much human history in this big, seemingly empty, land.

The plane dropped geographer Glen Macdonald's crew and I at Ennadai Lake to pull a pollen core from a small pond. Glen's graduate students would spend the winter reading the core in an ongoing attempt to understand the significance of tree line movement and global climate. Later, as we lay in the warm grass waiting for the plane to return and take us on to Angikuni Lake, it was hard to think of a more idyllic setting.

Departing the tree line for a final time, we flew north from Ennadai Lake, along the Kazan River to our base camp on the northeast corner of Angikuni Lake. Below, the tundra was a patchwork of bedrock exposures, muskeg bogs, sedge meadows and scattered pockets of stunted trees. Within a week, the spring so evident at Ennadai Lake, would bring leaves to the brown willows along the creeks and the green grass to the hills, but for now, the land was still in the grip of the last patches of snow. A few miles south of Angikuni Lake, the temperature dropped sharply beneath a threatening sky. We had flown past summer and almost outdistanced spring. Below, whitecaps and rafts of ice marked the spring breakup of rivers and lakes. Somewhere further south,

summer had officially started on June 21st. Here on the windblown Barren Lands, spring, that ever so brief transition between the depths of winter and the brief but brilliant summer, was still struggling to take hold.

As I jumped ashore, Len Robinson, the captain on the relief crew for the Twin Otter, wandered over from his tent and handed me a box of homemade chocolate chip cookies and a bottle of over proof Navy rum my wife Nancy had sent out on the plane from Yellowknife. I slid the cookies into my day pack and helped unload the plane before drift ice trapped it against shore. As the plane taxied out, I went in search of hot chocolate to thin the rum. A cap full of 180 proof can do wonders for industrial strength powdered chocolate or the insipid instant coffee someone had slipped into our rations.

As the rest of the canoe party landed over the next two days, the variable winds continued to shift the ice around the lake. Finally, the drift ice subsided during the night of June 30th. As it flowed out of Angikuni Lake into the Kazan River, waves of candle ice eroded from decaying bergs along shore and fell back into the water. The tinkle of the slender candle-like sliver of ice jiggling in the current, is as close as I have ever come to hearing the music of the spheres. I crawled out into the ever-present twilight of an Arctic midsummer night to sit by the river and listen to the ice.

Watching the dark waters of the Kazan River slip by at night, it is easy to imagine the river as a 500-mile ribbon of fast water connecting huge lakes. From the headwaters, to the central barrens—Snowbird, Kasba, Ennadai, Angikuni, Yathkyed, Forde,

Thirty Mile and Baker lakes form a vivid contrast to the fast flowing river. Rising in the boreal forest south of the tree line on the Northwest Territories' border with the Provinces of Manitoba and Saskatchewan, the Kazan River flows north along a winding course out of the trees, across the undulating Barren Lands to Baker Lake, at the geographic centre of Canada. In Baker Lake, the waters of the Kazan River mingle with those of the Thelon and Prince rivers before flowing east to meet Hudson's Bay in Chesterfield Inlet. Although the Kazan's drainage is the size of New York State, we saw only one other canoe party all summer.

From a fly fisherman's perspective, the Kazan provides tremendous opportunities ranging from quiet feeder streams, expansive lakes, and the endless variations of the untamed river. Comfortable fly-in lodges on lakes, high in the system south of the tree line, cater to lake trout fishing. Particularly, if you make arrangements ahead of time, they can also provide access to incomparable Arctic grayling water. Local, Baker Lake Inuit guides annually take a few fishermen 50 miles upriver to Kazan Falls, in late summer, by boat. And more recently, Ferguson Lake Lodge has opened an outpost camp on Yathkyed Lake. They are using a helicopter to fly sports around the central Kazan. That still leaves hundreds of miles of infrequently fished water on the Kazan River for fly fisherman with white water canoeing skills. A few canoe outfitters like Tom Faess of Great Canadian Ecoventures, now offer trips on the Kazan River so that descending it need not be a self-expedited trip.

Large lake trout and Arctic grayling can be taken throughout the short summer on fly tackle. The possibilities for entry to the Kazan are defined by what constitutes a good trip for you—lake trout and a comfortable lodge, roughing it with Inuit hunters, or the adventure of a lifetime following the river north as part of a small canoe party.

During those first few days at Angikuni, I had trouble believing my own advice. Although lake trout were being taken by others on spinners and spoons, I could not find the right fly. Despite my lack of initial success, I convinced myself that it was a good omen that my new rod cast tight loops into the biting wind. I knew fishing would improve as the water temperatures eased from the high 30s into the low 40s.

Over the last five days, summer has slowly crept further north onto the barrens. Sometimes it seems as though you can watch the advance and retreat of the summer as it battles its way north against the winds that sweep south across the Barren Lands from the Arctic Ocean. Since leaving Angikuni Lake on July 3rd, the weather has been extremely variable. Yesterday, we paddled into a head wind all day that blunted the current and raised whitecaps. By lunch, I began to doubt if I would ever be warm again. At mid-afternoon tea, everyone looked so despondent that I broke out Nancy's cookies to cheer them up. Though six days old, they were simply the best cookies within 500 miles. Before we set camp, my canoeing partner from Yellowknife, Mary McCreadie, amused and warmed our party by demonstrating how to centrifuge a bucket of coffee to settle the grounds. The visceral scream that accompanies a properly spun pot shocked our companions and broke out the first smiles of the day.

The next morning we awoke to a warm, calm, sunny day. To my surprise, our tents were stuck amid the stone circles of old Inuit tent rings and hunting blinds. Somehow in the rain, we had not noticed our ancient neighbours when we the pitched the camp. The discovery made the day seem even brighter as I walked along stone drive fences that had channeled caribou past ancient hunters as the herd surged toward the river.

After breakfast, I idled away a few minutes casting a Zug Bug in a small eddy. Last winter, preparing for a moment like this had caused me to reconsider my equipment. For years I had relied on a trusty 8-1/2-foot, 2-piece, 8 weight graphite rod for fishing the large rivers of the NWT. The rod is wonderful for three- to ten-pound lake trout, but it tends to overpower grayling. My childhood seven-foot, nine-inch stream rod was not long enough for the big water of the Kazan. With grayling on the brain, I began the search for a nine-foot, 5 to 6 weight, four-piece rod that would fit in a canoe pack. Fairly constant wind on the barrens, the need to mend a long line when fishing eddy margins, and the ability to handle large trout argued for a medium to fast action 6 weight. I was uncomfortable setting out with only one rod, but I felt compelled to pack as lightly as possible. Given my personal preference for medium action dry fly rods, I selected a four-piece travel rod with a hefty Full Wells grip. I mated the rod to a reasonably light 6 weight reel with a click drag. In retrospect, a reel that would have held additional backing would have been useful.

Later in the day, the low angle of the sun in the western sky caught the spray of the cascades as we portaged the first of three falls and ran down to the camp at the top of the second. Though Kazan Falls on the lower river is more famous, I believe that the Cascades are the most beautiful place on the river. As we ferried our canoes beneath the maelstrom of spray and rock of the first cataract, we could see the haze lofting above the horizon line of the second falls, a mere quarter of a mile below. Was it the power of the water that etched the place in my mind? I like to think it was the sun in the mist. We camped that night at the head of the mile-long portage around the third Cascade. (The next day the round "pack light, pack light" would became a mantra as I laboured under the weight of an 85-pound canoe or a 90-pound food pack. It was some comfort that all my fly gear weighted less than eight pounds.)

When everything two people need for seven weeks must be carried in four, 80-pound canoe packs and four day packs, sandwiched into a 17-1/2-foot prospector canoe, many niceties are left behind. Specialty lines fell into this category. For the sake of weight, I only carried a weight forward floating and a medium rate sinking tip line. Hindsight suggests floating and quick sinking shooting tapers would have been useful in many instances where consistently longer casts were necessary. I placed loops on the end of the fly lines so that I could easily replace terminal tackle and carry a selection of pre-tied leaders ranging from ones measuring five feet, steeply tapered for nymphing, to 11 footers for dry flies and small emerging nymphs. The selection was augmented by several small spools of tippet material. This solution proved slightly lighter and less bulky than carrying enough spools to totally rebuild worn leaders.

Can you leave home for a summer with only one box of flies? I tried, but in the end, I settled for four palm-sized aluminum boxes for regular use. As a reserve, I tucked in a stacked set of plastic containers filled with spare flies. Regrettably, loaded fly vests do not pack well and are a pain to wear over a life vest while paddling. After a lot of packing and repacking, the whole outfit fit into a medium-sized fanny pack that easily slid into the top of a canoe pack for portaging and quickly snapped onto a canoe thwart the rest of the time.

That evening Mary and I slipped down to the base of the second Cascade to fish. The canyon was a labyrinth of shadows and sunlight tossed about in the air by the mist. Water dashing into the rocks of the canyon made normal conversion impossible. The river's pulse surging free from the falls caused the eddies to rhythmically rise and fall three feet at a crack. The Arctic grayling we caught had brilliant red gills invigorated from the super-saturation of oxygen in the water. I had never recalled noticing the colour of a fish's gills before, as I lifted the fish from the water to slip the hook.

My approach for fishing the high volume, fast sections of the Kazan River was based on what I had learned travelling with the Mountain Indians in the Mackenzie Mountains—fish the big eddies along shore. By breaking a large river down into pieces, it is easier to learn the water and understand where the fish lie. I always begin my study of big water by exploring the 30-foot strip of flow adjacent to the bank. Even on a river a quarter of a mile across, the banks are still a really good bet. They have all of the ingredients essential for fish: cover, slower currents, and besides, they are terrestrial jackpots providing things such as ants and shrews. Look for quieter water tucked in and behind rock outcrops, small points and tributaries. If nothing is moving on the surface, drift nymphs and streamers increasingly deeper until you find where the fish are feeding. The bank allows a leisurely examination of the water with controlled drifts that become increasingly more difficult the further out into conflicting currents you cast.

Wading in 6 to 14 knot currents can be extremely hazardous. If you extend out too far, it is often impossible to wade back up the bar you descended only moments before. Once stuck on a bar, you are slowly sucked downstream and further out into the current. An alert guide, backed by the power of an outboard motor, and the stability of a broad beamed skiff, can generally rescue an overextended wader if they can be reached before being swept away. Canoes however, lack the ability to move up and hold at will in a swift current and thus make the rescue of a careless wader even more problematic. A betting man would not lay odds on your chances if you take a trip through the rapids on the Kazan River while wearing waders. Most of the time the river is too deep and the current is too fast to consider wading.

Over the last several days we have come down some incredible water. The current has tested everyone's skills, but we have done well. Many sections of the river are delightful to drift fish, but it is not a solo act. You require either a guide with a power skiff or a pair of paddlers handling the canoe in fast water. Drifting in a canoe can be extremely pleasant. By placing the fisherman in the middle of two paddlers, places can be fished that you cannot reach from shore. White water paddlers can slow the canoe below the speed of the current and allow the fisherman to drop a fly into promising holding water. The best action is often found by casting a pair of weighted nymphs along the bank as you drift by the rock bound shore.

It is odd to say that summer did not really bloom until July 10th. Remarkably, given that ice was still drifting downstream 10 days previous, the water temperature had risen to the point where that indomitable Scot, Richard Wilson went swimming. Later that evening, I found a school of Arctic grayling feeding on emerging mayfly nymphs along a quiet backwater. In the twilight, I could not distinguish more than the size of the hatch and so I fished a size 12 Adams parachute spinner with a bright white post, that I could see against the orange tinge of sunlight on the water. The ruse worked and I distracted several fish from the hatch. All of the grayling I caught were in the 3/4- to one-pound class. As I brought them to the beach, I slipped the hook and watched them dart back to the flooded stand of willows around which they had been feeding.

After a day spent walking the tundra doing archaeological surveying and ground truthing satellite imagery, I returned to the willows that evening to wait for the hatch. By the time the Arctic grayling started to rise, the sun was lying on the edge of the horizon at the beginning of its brief dip before

morning. I was still uncertain of the mayfly's hatching, so I imitated small stoneflies I found among the rocks at the waterline with a size 12 February Red. The next few minutes were spectacular fun. I missed as many strikes as I set and one large grayling snapped the 6X tippet. Finally, I landed a two-pound grayling. As the sun disappeared, the action slowed. Sporadic hits continued however in the afterglow of Arctic night until the sun again slipped above the horizon in the wee hours. Fishing became a daily ritual, played out under the low light of the Arctic evening.

The total collection of flies I dragged along is not as significant as the handful of truly successful ones that form the core of my northern fly box. Grayling are at their best when taken on a dry fly. The Kazan River is caddis country. I needed a durable, buoyant, and visible pattern for searching long eddy lines. The line is the watery seam between the river's current and the upstream rotation of the eddy. Fish hang out where water speed slows at the head and tail end of the line. I concentrated on finding a tough deer hair pattern that, with variations in size and colour, would cover the larger caddis. After a lot of experimentation, I decided on the Nelson's Caddis because it was easily tied with highly buoyant caribou hair which works very well for the wing. For that northern effect, I dubbed the body with caribou undercoat. On the river, it proved to be an excellent choice. Nelson's Caddis floats well in rough water, even after repeated strikes from grayling and small lake trout. Darker variations were hard to see in the shadows of late evening though. Under these conditions, I resorted to light winged versions with dark bodies, and double or single Humpys with light hackles, depending upon the size of the natural on the water. I carried Nelson's Caddis in sizes 8 through 12. For the smaller insects (sized 14 to 18) I relied on Humpys and Elk Hair Caddis. Most mayflies were effectively covered with variations of Adams dry and parachute patterns in sizes 12 to 16. Generally, the parachute was more successful. Grayling seem to like dry flies that hug the meniscus. This discovery has since led me to include a few Adams-like and Hendrickson no-hackles and Blue Wing Olive Paraduns. This broadens the mayfly selection to cover a range of grays, browns, and olives in a selection of sizes and shapes. Since there are no hatch charts for the Territories, and the fishing season is quite compressed, one must be ready to adapt to the unexpected. The most consistent grayling flies were, however, the Partridge and Orange soft hackle and the February Red Stonefly. An orange silk body with a dark brown clipped partridge soft hackle, ribbed with a fine gold wire and a black biot tail, the February Red extended the range of the simpler Partridge soft hackle. The Partridge and Orange was at its best when it was dead drifted in, or immediately under, the meniscus along the edge of the current. The February Red was particularly effective when used with a Leisenring lift at the end of the drift in quieter water where there was some up welling of the current.

Drift fishing required a very visible searching pattern. I used a size 10 Nelson's Caddis with a white wing or a light Humpy. Perhaps in the future, I would consider trying one of Gary Lafontaine's Dancing Caddis tied with a white wing. It is well suited to the rapid reflex fishing required when drifting large northern rivers.

It is impossible to fish the Kazan River and ignore lake trout. Low water temperatures mean that the lakers are available near the surface all summer. On the Kazan River I had the opportunity to take three- to five-pound lake trout on a dry fly, but more consistent results were obtained with nymphs and streamers. Before the trip, a friend gave me some multicolored gold and silver Muddler Minnows. While they lasted, the iridescent muddlers were my most consistent lake trout streamers. It was a sad night when I reached the end of my backing and I had to break off a trout I had never seen with my last silver muddler embedded in its jaw. Despite the effectiveness of the black with crystal flash Woolly Buggers, green with gold ribbed Matuka Streamers, and the standard muddlers that replaced the multicolored Muddler Minnows, they lacked a certain sparkle that seemed to make the other fly so deadly. Fishing the fast water I prefer nymphs tied in the round. The effect of more exact imitations is lost as they tumble along the bottom and the round nymphs are faster to tie, an important feature when you consider if you are not losing them, you are not fishing close enough to the bottom.

After a full day of archaeological surveying, and several stretches of white water, I slipped down to a huge eddy. Casting from a point halfway down the swirl, I worked 20 yards of line out to the edge of the heavy current and let it swing down the eddy before slowly retrieving the fly. On the third cast, the line stopped abruptly. I set the hook and started to work the fish, when I heard a crack by my ear.

Somehow I instinctively grabbed the rod as it slid down the line from the grip. Moments later, as I sat on a rock, contemplating the 38-day trip to Baker Lake without a fly rod, the multicolored Muddler Minnow floated up by my feet. July 12th lives in infamy.

There is a muse who looks after fly fishermen. By a long and torturous set of connections over the VHF radio, I got a message to Nancy in Yellowknife to put another rod on the resupply flight.

Over the next 16 days the weather continued to warm-up. From a high hill on July 15th, we could see that Yathkyed Lake, 10 miles to the north, was still full of ice. As we worked at a series of archaeological sites south of the inlet, the ice retreated day by day. Morning and evening, the hatches increased. During that time, I chose dozens of flies and mentally made millions of casts. There was little I could do but consider the tactics I would use when my trusty old 8 weight arrived. Fortunately, my companions with spinning rods provided fish for the pan as we rounded Yathkyed Lake.

Fishing the lakes along the Kazan provides an opportunity for testing your skills on large lake trout. Yes, there will still be rising pods of Arctic grayling along drop-offs and small lake trout near creek mouths, but they are not the prize of the lakes. Along fast sections of the river, four- and five-pound trout are common. In the lakes, fish in excess of 20 pounds lurk around the offshore reefs, points, and the inlet and outflow of the river. How you gear for and approach lake fishing will depend on your preferences and mode of transportation. Lodge based fishermen travelling with a boat generally have the latitude to carry a little more

fishing gear then the canoeist. Beyond the limitations of space, your definition of fly fishing will set the basic framework for your approach to lake trout.

If larger lake trout are your goal, then you will want to be able to go deeper with streamers. Work a full sinking line down 15 to 30 feet and then slowly retrieving it up the face of a reef. This method will generally produce some impressive results. This works well with big stonefly nymphs, weighted scuds, and a variety of streamers.

This will require an 8 or 9 weight rod and a reel with good drag and lots of backing. My preference is an 8 weight even though large weighted flies are a pain to cast. A heavier rod makes casting unwieldy nymphs and trolling streamers easier, but from my perspective, they are not as useful an all-around tool. It is not a choice between a 5 or 6 weight and an 8 or 9 weight, you should have one of each. I have discovered that while using a medium action rod, it is easier for me to develop a casting rhythm that controls the erratic flight of heavily weighted flies. I have successively gone through a series of rods ranging from eight-1/2 feet to nine-1/2 feet long. Longer rods are generally simpler to cast into the perpetual winds of the barrens and make working a line in conflicting currents easier.

Lake trout feed on plankton, freshwater sponges, crustaceans, aquatic and terrestrial insects, species of fish including smaller lake trout, and even small mammals. During our 1988 descent of the Kazan, I carried a variety of large sculpin patterns in a range of browns and greens, a variety of muddlers and matuka streamers, mayfly, caddis and stonefly nymphs and scuds in a variety of size and colour variations. Since that trip, I have worked on streamers that more closely imitate the nine spine stickle-backs; the slimy, spoonhead and deep water sculpin; and lake trout fry. These basic bait fish patterns will serve you well throughout the Territories. It is only a matter of time before an enter-prising angler creates a freshwater sponge pattern.

Lakes are often harder for the newcomer to read than a section of flowing water where the current gives clues to the structure of the streambed. Natural lakes, unlike reservoirs, do not have old topographic maps detailing the basin before submersion. A fish finder is unacceptable excess baggage on a canoe trip where portages demand you pack weeks worth of gear. Besides, recharging the batteries is impossible unless you are fishing near Baker Lake or at a lodge that is equipped with a generator. Guides working for the outfitters know the water they fish frequently. Beyond local knowledge, playing what-if? games with topographic maps may be your best clue to the underwater struc-ture of the large lakes along the Kazan. If you plan to paddle the river, you will have spent months reading the 1:250,000 (four miles = one inch) and 1:50,000 (1 mile = 1 1/4 inches) scale maps while planning your trip. It is standard procedure to use contour line crossings of the river as clues that may indicate major rapids or falls. Have you looked at them with an eye toward fish sheltering structures? If you are fishing out of a lodge, most operators will have a set of these maps hanging on the wall. Even better, they may have some aerial photographs.

Reading the slope of the land along shore, from the contour lines on the map, provides a clue to water depths near shore. Offshore drop-offs are very productive and are easily fished by canoes skirting the edge of a large lake. On a number of occasions, I have found large caddis hatching along a drop-off. The trick is to simply eliminate shallow, featureless sections of bottom as quickly as possible. Black crosses on the map, marking rocks and shoals in the lake, may denote under-water structures worth fishing with streamers. Railroad tracks are the strings of hash marks on contour maps which indicate a series of rapids. If the fishing has been slow out on the water, railroad tracks of rapids along a tribu-tary near the lake might indicate an excellent spot to stop and catch a few Arctic grayling for lunch.

The middle Kazan runs through the heart of one of the last holdouts of the great glaciers that once covered much of North America. Eskers, or the raised gravel beds of ancient streams that flowed beneath the glaciers, are marked on maps. Their sinuous trail in and out of the lakes can lead you to underwater bars that harbour fish. I remember paddling over a submerged esker in Baker Lake. A short distance below, large lake trout cruised along the edge of the bar. Unfortunately, my rod was packed for the long paddle across the lake, but I noted the spot on my map. Submerged eskers may be referred to by your guide as simply a "hot gravel bar". If you are travelling on your own, finding submerged eskers will be the result of some good detective work and luck on your part. Combine these observations with the location of the river and feeder streams, and you can start to create a list of places to checkout on the water.

When you arrive, look and see if any of the headlands you noticed on the map are actually bedrock outcrops that extend underwater to form a reef. The crystal-clear water of the Kazan system makes it relatively easy to checkout your theories in water of up to about 30 feet deep. Your knowledge base will build as you travel. Note bars, reefs and rock pinnacles that rise from the bottom on your map for later reference. If you take a minute, you may see trout hanging around the edges of these structures. After a few discoveries you will start to feel like a real Barren Lands fisherman who knows some secret spots the folks back home will never find.

Rounding the north side of Yathkyed Lake, we entered the land of the musk ox. At the mouth of the Nutarawit River, I plucked a large Ziploc bag full of quiviut (or musk ox wool) from the willows for dubbing. This fine oily fibre makes wonderful dry fly bodies. It dyes to lovely earthy tones.

Finally, on the 28th of July, after a long circumnavigation of Yathkyed Lake, we arrived at our food drop below the outlet. There, next to a food pack, was the tattered old rod tube with a note from Jim Raffan in Baker Lake, telling me the problems I had caused him. With the onset of twilight, I crept off to see if I could cast a 6 weight line on an 8 weight rod. Luckily, the system worked very well with longer lines. In fact, the 6/8 combination was a positive advantage when casting into the wind. Short casts were not great, but the jerry-rigged rod did roll cast well.

I admit it would have been easier if I had simply brought two rods and reels along, but I did learn an important characteristic of a Barren Lands

rod. It was the significance of being able to step down one or two line sizes in order to make working a long line into the wind easier. Along the Kazan River, I consistently needed to make 50-foot casts. Very frequently, I was confronted with a head wind. A long, 6 weight line nicely loaded my 8 weight rod, the smaller line diameter presented less drag and made casting into the wind easier. Not all of the 8 weights I have tried will step down as nicely as my old eight foot, six incher. Try the experiment at home before you make the final choice of rods for your trip.

That night, as a herd of 1,000 caribou wandered through our camp on their long trek south from the calving grounds, I knew I had seen the first sign that summer was waning. In the morning, the riverbank had a bathtub ring of caribou hair after the herd had forded on their way south.

With my heavier rod now in hand, I turned my attention from Arctic grayling to lake trout. Mastering the big eddy in deep and fast water is the secret to taking lake trout in large northern rivers. The most consistent techniques are variations of down and across presentations of heavily weighted nymphs, wet flies and streamers. I found that a two fly system with a nymph on the dropper and a streamer below produced my most consistent results.

Fishing large eddies, I typically take-up position on a gravel bar or rock outcrop at the head end. I make a short cast into the main current along the outside edge of the eddy. As the slack is pulled tight, I start to strip line off the reel at a rate that allows the fly to sink and naturally drift down the outside of the eddy. When the fly line reaches the far end, I use the rod tip to swing it out of the river current into the slack water. I slowly reel in line at a speed that imparts a swimming motion to the fly as it moves up the inside of the eddy. Strikes occur frequently as the fly is drawn from one side of the eddy line to the other. Watch at the end of the retrieve as the fly is picked up for the next cast. Strikes are common.

I have stressed working the line on and off the reel to reduce the most sensitive period of fighting a large fish on a fly rod, the time between the strike and when you have your retrieved any loose line onto the reel. With this technique, your initial cast is short, but you may feed nearly your whole fly line down the eddy line. If the strike occurs at the far end of the eddy, there will be a lot of line out, but very little slack. With a good drag and a tippet that will break before your backing knots, you should have a good shot at the fish and not lose your fly line. By slowly reeling in your retrieve instead of stripping the line by hand, when the strike occurs at the pickup, you will not have to try and fight the fish while struggling with gobs of loose fly line. The improved drags on modern fly reels make it possible to fight a large fish in big water when following it downstream is difficult or impossible.

As I swung the canoe beneath the point and across the current line into the backwater, I gasped, "What a fishing hole". The huge deep eddy was on river right, at the outlet of the wide spot, below Tyrrell Cliffs. It was formed by a long bedrock point that gently nudged out into a romping 8 knot current. The eddy behind it was a small harbour that slowly rotated against the river. After quickly assembling camp I slipped out of dinner preparations and raced to the point. A crude measurement with my fly line suggested that the eddy line was about 120 feet long. After futile attempts with bucktails and Marabou Streamers, I tied on my last silver multicoloured Muddler Minnow. On the lift following the end of the first cast, the reel began to scream. With the click drag on and the reel cranked all the way up, my palm was burning into the spool rim. I watched the end of the sinking tip and the backing knot disappear into the river. Before I could turn the fish and recover any line, the backing flew off the reel and then suddenly stopped as the spool parted the tippet 130 yards down river. As I retrieved my fly line, grateful all of the important knots held, I wondered how big the fish I had never seen really had been. Awhile later I landed a three- or four-pound fish that stretched dinner, but it was not the leviathan that got away.

On July 31 we entered Forde Lake. The upper end is less like a lake than a very wide river with a heavy current and rapids. The map makers must have been working off aerial photography taken during the winter, or the standing waves would have been obvious.

It was a cold and clear evening. Later, Orion faintly visible in the partially blackened sky, made me wonder if fly fishing exists in Valhalla to help mend warriors after a day of battle. Certainly the ale that flows so freely there would have been welcome at Forde Lake.

Since we had left the south end of Yathkyed Lake, there has been very little willow to burn in campfires. Though efficient, there is nothing cozy about sitting around a single burner camp stove. Looking for a diversion, Mary and I found a school of lake trout working a small eddy below the last rapids that bisected the "lake" before the real lake. Despite the fact that several fish were taken on spinners, I could not find a fly that worked. The world slowly transformed to orange and black in the final light of day. Finally, as everyone chilled and disappeared to bed, I tied on Hoagy Carmichael's Little Orange Mayfly. (Carmichael's fly is a small weighted orange yarn bodied streamer with a clipped white palmered hackle and a wood duck wing.) The fly seemed to pick up the light and shimmer as it sank out of sight. I worked the eddy from the midpoint, casting across the slack water to drop the fly just over the current line. After letting it settle for a few moments, I retrieved it into the eddy with several short jerks, picked it up and cast again further down the line. On the fourth cast, as the fly neared the tail of the eddy, it took a solid hit. After several downstream runs out into the current, the fish gave me a break and headed upstream. Recovering line, I slowly turned the fish and led a beautiful three-pound trout to the bank. As I slipped the hook from the fish's jaw, the last glimmer of the sun dropped below the horizon.

Paddling down Thirty Mile Lake, I watched trout rising off the weed beds. Except for a brief break during lunch, the rod had to stay tucked away while we clocked miles. Alas, though it is only the 4th of August, fall was in the air. After a long day on the water, a healthy serving of lake trout chowder and dumplings was a welcome treat. Fortunately, everyone was out taking a walk when I once again blew a dumpling through the valve on the pressure cooker. Hey, I was dis-tracted by a rising fish out beyond the canoes.

We portaged off Thirty Mile Lake through a small lake system that provided a pleasant walk across the tundra. The cataract at the end of the lake is incredible. Using the river left portage entails humping the canoes over some fairly large rocks. Mary made a good call when she picked the route through the small lake. During a well deserved break after the carry through the willows to the river bank, Jes Tate hooked a huge trout on his spinning rod in the eddy below the rapids. By skillfully using the current and holding on the bottom, the fish deprived Jes of even a glance of his adversary. After a protracted stalemate, the line parted on a rock. Though it was only the 8th of August, we had to begin thinking about where to camp by late afternoon. Gone were the long halcyon days around the summer solstice in late June and early July when one could travel at will, day or night.

After a very brief paddle, we camped on the outside of the bend below the falls. Working the outside of an eddy with a palmered variation of Greenwell's Glory, I took a heavy strike. By the time the fish's run had reached the far end of the eddy line, I was able to bring him across and finish the fight in the slack water. I must be getting better, there was still a little fly line left on the reel. The six-pound cock became a key ingredient for one of Mary's camp specialties. Her fish cakes are a blend of lake trout, corn meal, whole wheat flour, Worcestershire sauce, curry powder, garlic, and a few secret herbs. Garnished with Tabasco sauce, and served with a side of pasta and brown "industrial grade" sauce mix, dinner was a success. Over coffee, while Mary and Annie Roberts made fudge, Jes fussed it was a shame to turn a trout into fish cakes but, "my were they good".

The trip is starting to wane now. It is August 10th. We are camped by the lip of Kazan Falls about 30 miles from Baker Lake. From the rim, the Kazan River hurdles about 120 feet down into a craggy limestone canyon. Along the river, below the falls, the eddies surge 6 to 12 feet. I am sure there were Arctic grayling hanging around, but with that swell I could not figure out how to keep the fly in the water—let alone make a decent presentation. On my way out of the canyon, I met ornithologist Judith Kennedy making her way toward a falcon nest. The ledges of the gorge are a favoured nesting habitat of the peregrine.

Portaging around the falls is a trek across a mile-wide boulder field. On the bright side, it is generally downhill and it was not raining so the rocks were not slippery. Below the falls, the river briefly flattens. In the warm sun, a school of grayling were bobbing for emerging nymphs along a weed bed. The swirls of the fish and the slice of the paddles were the only breaks in the mirrored surface of the river. The respite, however, was brief. Around

the first bend, the Kazan River starts building speed for its turbulent run to Baker Lake. Before long I calculated, based on map distance and time, that the canoes were ripping along at about 8 knots. As Jes—the resident yachtsmen—tore by, I yelled my revelation. He shook his head, and yelled back, "I can't believe it, by my calculation the hull speed of 17-1/2-foot prospector canoe is 5 to 6 knots. We must be hydro-planing." Through standing waves and around bends we tore. Finally, compelled by the onset of evening, we took a chance on a campsite by a creek and swung the canoes into the relative calm of a big eddy. As the boats bumped the beach everyone was buzzing with excitement.

It was to be our last night on the Kazan. Anticipating the retrospective mood of the group, I slipped off to the river. I walked down a small tundra creek that wound its way through the high ice scoured banks to the main flow of the Kazan. Immediately above its mouth, a long gravel bar pushed the current out to form a long eddy, In the heavy current, I watched larger grayling dimple the surface. Under the stars, I picked my way back to camp to finish the last dram of over proof in my cocoa.

Tributary of the upper Kazan River.

Photo by John Gierach

Arctic Grayling.

Photo by John Gierach

Chapter Four

Tree River—The Trip That Could Have Been

It hit a high of -62 degrees F. today. In the short burst of sunlight and the protracted twilight which we call day during January in Yellowknife, I spent hours outside installing a heated blanket on the propane tank in an effort to keep it vaporizing. Thank God for the wood stove or the house would have frozen.

Later, huddled over the stove, with a hot toddy in hand, the only thought that came to my numbed mind was fishing for Arctic charr. Eight years and seven winters in the Territories and I have only been charr fishing once. (Actually there were only a few precocious grilse coming in. The charr run was not happening.) Despite that experience, fishing the Tree River for Arctic charr is like angling for brook trout in the Nipegon River before Ontario Hydro built its dam. Tree River and Arctic charr easily come out in the same mouthful. By reputation, the Tree is where the big charr run.

Situated 300 miles north of Yellowknife, the Tree River flows north into the Arctic Ocean east of the community of Coppermine. The sport fishery was pioneered by Plummer's Lodge which flies guests in from the main camp on Great Bear Lake. Over the years their sports have compiled an impressive record of success on the Tree River. If you pop into Skinners Sport Shop in downtown Toronto and mention Arctic charr, a clerk may casually comment that Peter Pocklington, owner of the Edmonton Oilers, was in last week and reported they were hitting red and yellow sea duces. The Tree River is as famous as Arctic waters get.

Living in the north precluded the sensible solution, booking a trip with Plummer's. Real Arctic men organize their own adventures—no question about it.

Labour Day, after the lodge has closed for the season, is considered to be the best weekend by the locals. It is when northerners book their charter aircraft. I briefly weighted the economics of scale, a small intimate party of three or four friends on a single engine Beaver versus 11 to 12 acquaintances on a larger Twin Otter. Economics rule the world—the dollars and cents only made sense if the price was reduced to a few hundred dollars a head. The Twin Otter won, oh well, it is a relatively big river. Early the next morning, I called Air Tindi and booked the flight. I wanted lots of time to sell the seats.

While my wife Nancy was still wondering who was going to pay for the plane, I began ruminating about a new rod. I was sure that my eight year old, 8 weight would do the job, but these were Arctic charr, I was going to the Tree River, a second rod was a necessity. After misadventures on the Kazan River, I could not fly off to the top of the world with only one heavy rod. Historically speaking, this was prior to the real blossoming of high quality of 4-piece rods on the market. In those days, for my money and casting rhythm, the best you could get came from a little shop in Stowe,

Vermont. I had been using their 5 and 6 weight, 4-piece rods for several years and so the choice came naturally. Having spent years stuffing rods into float planes and helicopters, the new 8 weight stick had to be a 4-piece unit. To cast well and fight hard, the grip had to fit naturally into my hand. Custom cork meant custom rod. Hey, this is charr fishing, you need the right equipment. By the time the cold snap broke, a new rod was on the way.

From that moment on I have thought constantly about a trip I have yet to make. I sold all my seats on the plane before the Canadian Department of Fisheries and Oceans closed the Tree River for the season, after its yearly quota had been reached. Pneumonia then struck two of us on our return from Great Bear Lake before we could regroup and go to another secret spot down the coast from the Tree. After a reorganization the next year, I hurt my back unloading a 55-gallon drum of gas from a boat on Great Bear Lake. Momentarily deterred, I let the Tree River settle in the dust while we moved to Colorado.

Thoughts of that river will simply not leave me alone. This summer Dale Freschi, a Canadian national fly fisherman who formerly lived in Hay River, spent an evening reeling me in with his home videos of Arctic charr on the Tree. Several beers later, we were in his basement digging out the big sculpin patterns that match the creatures that swim around in the river. Through spats of both clear and dirty water in the river, Dale has consistently scored big using long shanked size 2 imitations of the slimy sculpin in a range of colours from brown to olive green.

Dale, a fall regular on the Tree River, regaled me with tales of the year that nobody was catching fish on the west side of the river. He and his brother inflated their float tubes and paddled to the other bank and scored.

The downside of a fall trip to the Tree is that it is very cold and generally raining. If the weather comes in hard, you are stuck in a little mountain tent weighted down with rocks to keep it from blowing away. Weather conditions do suggest doing the trip with Plummer's during the brief Arctic summer when they have their spacious wall tents up, a regular source of heat to dry out with, and plenty of food.

When I turned down an invitation to go to the Tree River this fall, after "she who must be obeyed" suggested it was time to come home, I remembered my Tree River jinx. Just because I left home in May for a two-week contract, that extended itself into a four-month tour of the NWT, why should I miss the Tree River again? Justice is illusory.

We had our first big snow in the Colorado high country this morning. Shortly it will be time to start planning for next season. Maybe this year I should simply call Plummer's, it would at least be a different approach. As I ponder my options, I leave you with my yearly mantra, "Next year the Tree."

Chapter Five

A Land of Rocks, Lakes and Trees

Contemplating a fishing trip on the Canadian Shield brings back a thousand memories of the rocks and trees lining tranquil lakes and rushing rivers across half a continent. As a boy, I learned to portage canoes over endless shield rock between the countless lakes and creeks of Algonquin Park in northern Ontario. Along the way I got to know speckled trout that had largely disappeared from my home waters in western New York. Later, the waters of the Hayes River in northern Manitoba and Ontario's Spanish River made permenant impressions on my psyche. Year by year as I wandered further north, it was always the rolling rocks of the Canadian Shield, the cry of the Arctic loon and the splash of the paddle that played on my soul. As a young archaeologist, I travelled northern Quebec's giant Caniapiscau River with the Cree, before Hydro-Quebec had its way. Perhaps it is the memory of the giant speckled trout in the rapids above the old Eaton Canyon Club that first drove home the values at risk in careless development. North of the 60th parallel, whether it is the relatively accessible water of the Yellowknife River north of Great Slave Lake, or the distant Coppermine River, shield country provides some of the best fishing in the Northwest Territories.

When I ruminate about the boreal forest, I remember a day when I was paddling with Anna Canada, near the Cree community of Oxford House in northern Manitoba. We were plugging our way up the Red Sucker River to look at a rock painting, when I quite unexpectedly exclaimed, "You know all black spruce don't look alike". She giggled and allowed as how I had been in the north too long. Despite the homogeneity that strikes many people on their first visit to the boreal forest, the Canadian Shield is a wonderfully diverse place that is full of nooks and crannies that beg to be explored.

Shield rivers are swift flows that connect lakes. They combine a blend of quick smooth runs and white water which plunge into pools that beg to be fished. Eddying out of the fast water into a tranquil lake provides time to reflect on the day. The continuous runs of rapids on the Beaulieu River look like railroad tracks on the topographic map. With a good trip report and reasonable white water skills, you can pick your way through. Carrying the canoe around the impassable bits— over bedrock exposures and through muskeg bogs is an expression of independence. There is literally nowhere I cannot go on the Shield if I have a pack, a canoe, and a fishing rod. If you can wiggle a boat or a canoe far enough along any shield river to escape the highway, you are apt to find fish.

Evenings I used to sneak out of Yellowknife to small lakes near the Ingraham Trail and float my canoe along the edge of a bog. Beavers and muskrats swam back and forth. Cranes' tracks lined the shallow water near the shore and the sandpipers dawdled near the edge. The quiet would only occasionally be shattered

Dale Freschi with a northern pike on the North Arm of Great Slave Lake.

when a pike would streak out from under a lily pad to smash my popper.

Fishing further afield in unfamiliar shield country, I looked for osprey nests. The big birds seek a commanding view of a lake narrows or river runs that provides them with a regular supply of fish. It is a trick I learned while flying the old power line from Snare River to Yellowknife with biologist Chris Shank. The osprey had built their nests on towers that overlooked lake narrows. Circling raptors have often led me to whitefish, Arctic grayling, and northern pike.

A wilderness fishing trip, on one of the rivers that empties into Great Slave Lake, is easy to accommodate in a busy schedule. A lot of angling and paddling can be done in two or three weeks. If that does not strike your fancy, there are a number of lodges on the Shield that will cater to the fly fisherman. The following is not a complete list or an endorsement of any establishment, it is simply a sampler designed to give you a taste of what is available for fly fishermen from the tree line to the Alberta border.

True North Safari's MacKay Lake Lodge is famous for lake trout, Arctic grayling, whitefish and caribou. Situated an hour by air from Yellowknife, along the edge of the tree line in the upper Lockhart River drainage, MacKay Lake Lodge offers a combination of river and lake experiences. It is also a jumping off point for very secluded outpost camps on Aylmer Lake and the Snake River.

Enodah Wilderness Travel's lodge on Trout Rock Island in the North Arm of Great Slave Lake is a big lake experience at the edge of the Shield. Enodah is situated virtually on the western corner of the Canadian Shield. It is only a short hop by air from Yellowknife to great northern pike water.

Taiga Tours's Thebacha Bed and Breakfast in Fort Smith, and Large Pike Lake Camp southeast of town on the Alberta border are situated in the heart of the boreal forest. Master guide Clayton Burke can arrange tours of Wood Buffalo National Park to compliment your fishing trip. Their fly-in camp specializes in northern pike and whitefish.

While these lodges will give you a taste of the area, there are in fact twenty-some lodges on the Canadian Shield in the NWT— each with its own attractions.

Chapter Six

Great Slave Lake

Great Slave Lake is available, yet remote. Road access at Hay River, Frank's Channel off the Mackenzie Highway, and at Yellowknife, open only a small portion of the lake for casual use. Most of the fifth largest lake in North America is still only accessible by float plane or extended boat trip. A combination of approaches make a myriad of angling opportunities possible. They range from an afternoon of northern pike fishing with Morris Rabesca from Sah Naji Kwe Camp near the Frank's Channel Bridge, to a week split between angling for pike near Enodah Lodge on the North Arm, and pursuing lake trout and Arctic grayling from Trophy Lodge on the East Arm.

Before gold strikes triggered the founding of the city of Yellowknife in the late 1930s, the ancestors of the Yellowknives had exploited the fish runs of Yellowknife Bay for generations. Their ancient fish camps stretched from the mouth of the Yellowknife River to Gros Cap. Cached, dried fish were an important hedge against the uncertainties of winter. The early fur traders followed their example and established "Old" Fort Providence southeast of the modern Yellowknives' community of Dettah. Built for Alexander Mackenzie in 1796, the post served as a fishery for Northwest Company operations on Great Slave Lake. Today there is a floating fish plant off Wool Bay only a few miles from the ruins of the fort. The plant and the fish camps scattered near it underscore the continued significance of the commercial fishery along the north shore of Great Slave Lake.

The islands of the north shore archipelago spread from Dettah to Gros Cap at the entrance to the East Arm. They are glacially polished Precambrian granite domes tufted with spruce and aspen. Their twisting shores offer protected coves for boats and expanses of clear rock that make casting painless. Below the surface, the undulating rock has created wonderful fishy structures that occasionally remove the bottom end from an outboard motor. Local Yellowknife guides from the Deton'cho Corporation can help you find lake trout, northern pike, Arctic grayling, and whitefish among the islands without the pain of learning the waters.

When I met Steve and Louise Matthews at Yellowknife's Wildcat Cafe for breakfast, Louise and I exchanged our customary joke about pack horses. Years ago when I worked for the Prince of Wales Northern Heritage Centre, Louise had been the department finance officer who had reviewed an invoice for a string of pack horses I had blithely attached to a travel advance. I subsequently disappeared back into the field on another project while fur flew in Yellowknife. By the time I returned, someone had decided that horses were the same as renting a boat and I was almost forgiven. Thank heavens I never asked permission, forgiveness was hard enough to come by.

When Steve had a chance to break in on our revelry, he quietly suggested an afternoon fishing trip to Wool Bay. Household tasks aside, it was Father's Day and he wanted to try out his new fly rod. Although Steve and I were set on Arctic grayling, Louise suggested that it would be nice if we brought home a big northern pike for dinner. On the way down Yellowknife Bay, Steve described his favourite method for filleting pike to remove all of the bones. He then uses the groove left in the flesh from cutting the lower row of bones out to insert stuffing when he bakes the pike in foil. It was obvious Louise planned for Steve to prepare the barbecue.

In deference to the threat of small craft warnings, Steve and I stopped at an island only a few miles past Dettah. If we had gone on to the more protected waters near Wool Bay, it would have been easy to miss a change in the wind. There would be other gentler times for pushing on to more distant waters.

The rock pools, in the lap of the waves, contained a mixture of black stonefly nymphs (size 2X to size 8), a few tan caddis (size 18), and the prerequisite number of midges (size 18 and size 20). Stoneflies crawling up the rocks to emerge were the hatch of the day. I had encountered the same fly, four weeks earlier, south of Great Slave Lake along the Kakisa River. Spring on the north shore is retarded by the slow retreat of the ice from the centre of the lake. Swarms of dragonflies were darting through the air eating mosquitoes on the wing. Wind gusts downed the "mosquito hawks" that turned too tightly near the water, making them the afternoon's only dry

fly activity. When Steve watched a grayling come up and nose the same struggling dragonfly twice before it turned away, it was obvious that the fish were not really interested. If the grayling had been feeding so heavily that they were too full for struggling dragonflies, they had to be feasting on stonefly nymphs.

Rigging for the bottom, Steve chose a full sinking line while I slipped on a sinking tip. We both used 6 weight rods to turn the weighted nymphs. Imitating the slender black stonefly required a sparse pattern. I chose a clipped Woolly Worm with a split goose quill tail that gave the correct general impression, while Steve selected a very thin Black Muddler with a sparse wing that imitated the profile. Sinking the flies we worked them slowly up the rocky shore along the path of the naturals. The exercise was rough on flies and attracted no grayling. We fished the mid-water with attractor patterns, but nothing happened. The bluster had pushed a smorgasbord of drowned insects from the windward shore, but no grayling were feeding in the eddies at the ends of the island where the flotsam and jetsam rafted out of the wind. I changed to a more exacting imitation. When that failed, we tried one of Steve's favorite tricks and fished the windward side where the grayling collect to feed on food stirred up by the waves. Switching to a floating line, I worked a dry fly over shallow shoals near shore, while Steve retrieved his spinning rod to try for a pike. In the end, we did not even get a pike for Louise.

Later at the dock in Yellowknife, we heard a few "you should have been there yesterday" stories. Bill Cody complained about fog along the ice edge out near the West Mirage Islands.

Not even ardent spin fishermen really wanted to talk about Arctic grayling. Undaunted, on the way up the path to the house, Steve and I mused about the terrific dry fly action we would find in a few days when the stoneflies emerged from their nymphal shucks. Arctic grayling can be as picky as snotty South Platte River browns that turn and fin away from a fly one size too large. Fortunately, our Father's Day experience is not the rule, fishing south of Dettah is generally very good.

A few days later, as I chatted with Ragnar Wesstrom, he casually let it drop that he had guided Michigan angler, Herb Noffert, into enough Arctic grayling and northern pike that he had sworn off Alaska. They struck pay dirt a couple of miles from where we were skunked. One evening later in the week, I walked in from the Dettah Road to the far shore of Yellowknife Bay looking for northern pike. I resoundingly connected with a Red and White Bunny Fur Streamer off a weed bed. It is a simple pattern. A long white rabbit tail, a red body wrapped with heavy copper wire—to retard chewing—and a couple of turns of saddle hackle mated to a long, size 2 streamer hook. They take two minutes to tie and will, with luck, last through a few savage raps by a pike.

Angling pressure around Yellowknife has increased since Gerry Wolfe and I used to go down to Wool Bay after pike in the early 90s. As the water quality has improved, there seem to be more lake trout in Yellowknife Bay than there have been for many years. Despite concern for the Yellowknife River Arctic grayling run, fishing for grayling around the north shore islands is still good. Quantities of healthy northern pike lurk near town. If the move toward

catch and release continues to grow with Yellowknife sportsmen, the sports fishery should remain strong.

Yellowknife is a hub for air and water traffic to the East Arm of Great Slave Lake. The inside passage through the islands is accessible to boaters who know the water, but shoals make the trip through the archipelago to the East Arm treacherous for the uninitiated. Larger crafts follow the shipping channel across the main body of the lake. Travel on the outside, however, is exposed and subject to changes in the weather. It is not uncommon to find boats from Yellowknife at Fort Reliance on the far end of the East Arm.

The East Arm is big water. Vertical cliffs on Red Cliff Island soar hundreds of feet above the arm, while the lake plunges into subterranean canyons several thousand feet deep. (It is deeper than Great Bear Lake and Lake Superior.) The fishing is spectacular but it takes more than a summer vacation to learn the water. Your best bet is to go through a lodge. Trophy Lodge at Fort Reliance is a short boat trip from the mouths of the Lockhart and Hoar Frost rivers. Frontier Lodge, by the mouth of the Snowdrift River, has exceptional Arctic grayling, northern pike and lake trout fishing. Both are accessible by air from Yellowknife. The Katseyedie River near Plummer's Lodge produced the all tackle record for Arctic grayling. The trophy was 29 7/8 inches long and weighed five pounds, 15 ounces. Guests regularly take trophy northern pike and lake trout in addition to the Arctic grayling. Plummer's Lodge has direct weekly air service from Winnipeg, Manitoba.

East Arm sports fishing is largely based on trolling for lake trout with hardware. Despite this, all of the lodges have excellent opportunities to take Arctic grayling, northern pike and whitefish on the fly. Early in the season lake trout can be apprehended near the surface with streamers and occasionally on dry flies.

The Lockhart River rises near Jolly Lake, northeast of the city of Yellowknife, and wends its way through Courageous, MacKay, Aylmer, Clinton Colden and Artillery lakes on its way to join Great Slave Lake near Fort Reliance. The haunts of the upper Lockhart River are famous among Barren Land fishermen. The last leg of the river from Artillery Lake down to Great Slave Lake is so turbulent that most canoeists prefer to make the three-mile trek over Pikes Portage rather then lug their gear down the river.

Without a 100-pound pack, it is worth the four-mile trek up the bank of the Lockhart River to see Parry Falls. Twisting through a rock keyhole, the river squirts from a cliff and rolls off the canyon wall below. Huge standing waves fill the gorge as the Lockhart struggles to regain its composure.

Early in 1834, after wintering at "Old" Fort Reliance, Captain George Back and his crew dragged their long boats up the Lockhart River, on their way to the first European descent of the Great Fish River. From Chantrey Inlet on the Arctic coast, Back returned upriver and sailed back down the Lockhart to winter again at Fort Reliance. The Great Fish was subsequently renamed for Back. The chimneys at Back's winter quarters are an enduring historic landmark to the age of Arctic exploration. Located at MacLeod Bay, a few hundred yards from the mouth of the Lockhart River, the walk to the ruins of the fort is a good excuse to stretch your legs.

The shoals of MacLeod Bay and the lower Lockhart River are blue ribbon water in a region known by anglers for good fishing.

At the mouth of the river, a brisk 7 or 8 knot current ripples the final run of the Lockhart with small standing waves. Staring down into the river you see fish far below in the crackling clear flow. I remember sliding my Polaroid glasses up and down my nose, trying to get the picture in perspective. Ten or twelve feet down, there were trout and grayling holding in pockets along the bottom. I could see them nose up to grab morsels that drifted by. So clear, so close, yet were those fish obtainable with a slow sinking tip line and lightly weighted flies?

Travelling in the north, the size of one's creel is limited by the space available on small planes. My 8 weight rod would stand the task of bringing a hefty lake trout up through the current, but could I get down and drift a deceptive tidbit past those scour pocket dwellers? As a compromise to space, I had only brought floating and medium density sinking tip lines with me. All my weighted nymphs and streamers were lightly leaded, none were real sinkers. My frustration grew as my partner George Pellissey took trout after grayling with a heavy spoon, while I watched the current drift my flies well above the fish. With a mitt full of split shot clamped to my leader, a pair of nymphs would almost lay out and drift along the bottom. Whenever I thought I had a good run started, however, the fly line would become hydrodynamic at the wrong moment and soar the flies off the bottom.

Photo by John Gierach

Lake trout.

George finally suggested that I attach a trolling sinker to the end of my fly line. In honor of his invention, he took the first cast. Actually cast is a misnomer, I pitched the lead and leader out into the current and the fly line followed. George drew a strike on a size 2 Mickey Finn during the first drift. The weight at the end of the line was so heavy, however, that he could not keep pressure on the fish as the leader quaked like a string tied to a post in a windstorm. With the point proven, he grabbed a hacksaw from the boat box and cut the weight in half. The revised contraption actually hooked lake trout with fair regularity. Arctic grayling seemed to hit too softly for me to feel the take with all the pressure on the tackle.

When I got back to Yellowknife, I ripped open Dan Bailey's catalogue and ordered another spool, a high density full sinking line and a handful of lead heads. At the bench I created an assortment of very heavy nymphs, including some brassies that require a hard-hat when you cast them. Later, I had another shot at the mouth of the Lockhart. I found, much to my satisfaction, that I could tumble a fly along the bottom, fight a fish and actually call it fly fishing. When that infrequently used line wears out, I think I will replace it with a running line and shooting heads. The combination will give me more flexibility. The thin running line will belly less in a heavy current and I can carry specialty items like a lead core head without wasting an entire spool.

The narrow inlet from the mouth of the river to MacLeod Bay provides more gentle fishing. Low water temperatures and steep loose gravel drop-offs make a boat preferable to wading.

Working a sinking tip line with nymphs and small streamers for Arctic grayling provided a pleasant diversion while I waited for a hatch of caddis to start a rise. With less press from the current, it is easy to fish the top 10 feet of the bay. When the grayling are not rising, they are frequently in the shallows nibbling caddis and stonefly nymphs or chasing small nine spine sticklebacks and sculpins.

Out on the open waters of MacLeod Bay the feeling is different. Large open fetches make wind and rough water a challenge. The lake trout require sinking lines and trolling flies. Grayling are available around creek mouths and in the Hoar Frost River northeast of Fort Reliance.

Somewhere north of Great Slave Lake's Taltheilei Narrows, the engine on the left side of the Twin Otter lost power. I turned and quietly asked George if he knew that Otters flew nicely on one motor. Quizzically, he looked through me at the feathering propeller. Before he could utter a sound, the co-pilot stuck his head through the bulk head and told us we were going to put down on a small lake. Apparently, the airline was sending a Turbo-Beaver out with an engineer to look at the Otter. Before he turned back to the controls, however, our fearless aviator concluded that there was nothing to worry about, they had picked a lake with great fishing.

Single Otter unloading at MacKay Lake Lodge.

Photo by Gary Jaeb

Chapter Seven

Trout Rock

I had spent the last two weeks working on the environmental impact statement of a hot diamond property. I was babbling, tired and grumpy. My condition was obvious when I came home to pack for the weekend and discovered I had lost my sleeping bag. Somewhere in one of the tiny Northwest Territories communities of Wha Ti, Edzo, or Deline that damn bag is lying in a corner. I still have no recollection of its loss. Fortunately, as I was contemplating my stupidity, Tom Andrews called to wish me a big fish and ended up offering to loan me a bag which I picked up on my way to the float plane. I was in need of a courageous foe, northern pike fishing on the North Arm of Great Slave Lake promised a fair fight.

Perched on a series of rolling granite domes, Enodah Lodge has a picturesque view of the archipelago from the corner of Trout Rock Island. The country is quiescent Canadian Shield. Across a narrow channel from camp, the north shore of Great Slave Lake twists through a labyrinth of small granite reefs and shallow channels. Glacially polished outcrops, rimmed with birch, pine and spruce, overlook countless lakes and ponds. It is the patchwork rock on the Canadian Shield that immediately distinguishes it from the Mackenzie Low Lands across from the north shore.

Below the surface of Great Slave Lake, the granite slowly slips under the muck until it disappears back into the earth's crust beneath the North Arm. These Precambrian rocks do not reappear again until they pop-up in the lower levels of the Grand Canyon thousands of miles to the south.

On a clear day, the glint of White Beach Point is visible across the North Arm, from Trout Rock Island. It marks the beginning of the Mackenzie Low Lands. By contrast to the Canadian Shield on the north shore, the southwest shore is dominated by a succession of gravel beach ridges that mark the transformation of Great Slave Lake from its predecessor—glacial Lake McConnell. At the height of the ice retreat, around 10,000 years ago, Lake McConnell covered the basins of Lake Athabasca, Great Slave Lake and Great Bear Lake. The gravel strands of ancient shorelines rise gradually inland, until one of the high beaches forms the roadbed for the Mackenzie Highway on its route from Fort Providence to the community of Edzo. To the south, the Mackenzie Wood Bison Sanctuary lies within the old lake basin.

Half drooped against the window of an old Single Otter, I watched Yellowknife disappear as we slipped the bonds of town to head out across the patchwork of rocks and trees. The airframe plate on the bulkhead in front of me revealed that the plane was built the year after I was born. In the distance, dust trails on the Mackenzie Highway tapered off toward Rae and Edzo. Enodah Lodge is remarkably close to Yellowknife and yet totally isolated. The half-hour flight from Yellowknife passes over the reefs of the North Arm archipelago that protect the water from causal users. Learning the convoluted channels of the North Arm is not a weekend activity. Lifelong residents still lose propellers and engines to forgotten rocks. As a result, you can be alone with one of Enodah's guides on some of the best pike water in Great Slave Lake, a few air miles from town. As I stepped off the float at camp, I needed all the distance I could get from town to disconnect and fish away the previous two weeks.

The weekend promised to be a real treat. Dale Freschi was along as the pike coach. After watching his fluid casts and listening to his practical fish sense, I resolved again to practice more. As Dale checked gear and helped install steel pike leaders, Ragnar Wesstrom, owner of Enodah Lodge, and I chatted about Trout Rock.

Trout Rock Island has been a Native Yellowknives' encampment for hundreds of years. The Hudson's Bay Company operated a small post near the island in the mid-1920s. Teepees, rectangular canvas wall tents, and sod roofed cabins gave way to a "modern" log cabin village in the 1940s when the Canadian Government provided lumber for floors and shingles for roofs. During the 1950s the community had a Catholic church and a Protestant Sunday School. When a winter tractor road reached the rock in the 1960s, people gradually moved into the Dogrib village at Fort Rae and the Yellowknives' Dene communities of N'dilo and Dettah near Yellowknife. Trout Rock is now a seasonal hunting camp.

Enodah Lodge is a neatly built tent camp around Paul Drygeese's log cabin. Ragnar's wife Doreen grew up in the house. Big white canvas wall tents with permanent frames and spacious plywood decks provide bright, bug-free sleeping accommodations. The dining tent is a comfortable space for rehashing the day. Doreen's uncles Frank Drygeese and Jonas Noel are now the island's only permanent residents. They guide for the lodge in the summer and trap in the winter.

By the late 1940s, fishing pressure had pushed lake trout out of the shallows of the North Arm leaving behind a spectacular northern pike fishery. The Arm was marginal habitat for the trout, but remains perfect for pike, whitefish and walleye.

Northern pike action on the North Arm is slow in the morning until the chill wanes and life in the weed beds kicks into gear. A nine o'clock start fit the moods of old friends who talked over a few beers until the pre-dawn lighting of the sky chased everyone to bed. In the morning after breakfast, Frank Drygeese loaded Greg Cook from Yellowknife and myself, into his skiff and we headed slowly toward the narrows at Drygeese Bay. A few minutes later I hooked my first pike, in front of Frank's log cabin, a few hundred yards from the lodge. In the next boat, a few minutes later, Dale took a walleye on a red fat head minnow. Working the weed beds of Drygeese and Francois bays, Frank got both Greg and I into nice fish.

Greg fished a neutral density line. I stuck with a floating one. We both installed steel pike tippets on our 8 weight rods. Unless you are after a class record, the steel leader allows you to fight the fish harder and release them more quickly. Greg started the morning with a black Fat Head minnow, as I clamped on a black Mega Diver with a red crystal flash tail. Both flies improved after they had been liberally chewed by a couple of pike. After a particularly big pike chomped through his steel leader, Greg changed to a red Fat Head. The floating line was a good compromise for me. It eased casting bulky deer hair flies, as long as I let the terminal tackle sink down three or four feet. The pike hung near the base of the weed beds. Occasionally, a pike would boil to the surface if you tugged a small hair mouse over its lair, but generally we had to let a water logged diver sink to a five count before starting a fast retrieve. Austin Marshall from Yellowknife was using a full sinking line to its full advantage. When we met him in Francois Bay, he was having such a fine time that he did not even rise to my joke about the pike biting his fly out of professional courtesy to a lawyer.

In retrospect, I should have strung two rods, one with a floating, the other with a sinking tip. This would also facilitate fishing multiple fly patterns. With a steel tippet, changing the fly demands a pair of pliers to mash and straighten the tiny cable connector. As a consequence, I did not take time to experiment with many flies as long as the current victim produced fish at a steady rate. The worse the diver looked, the better the pike liked it.

An unassuming fisherman, Greg quietly took the biggest fish that came to our boat. He started his run with a modest pike. It was 39 inches long with a girth of 16 1/2 inches. Using the pike weight formula of length * girth 2/800, we figured it was an honest 13-pound fish. Greg and Dale debated the proper measurement of big fish at lunch, after Dale released a 40-inch beast with an 18 inch girth. Dale's fish had a formula weight of 16 or more

pounds and actually tipped the scales at 17 pounds. After much discussion, they decided they liked the weight measurements derived by laying the fish flat on a damp piece of plywood, rather then when it is held up. The girth is larger and therefore the calculated weight of the fish, more closely approximates the actual weight of a pike hung in a sling on the spring balance.

My fish karma that day had little to do with the "big" ones. I was quite content to steadily catch and release fish between three and eight pounds. While the discourse on big fish continued, I took a nap for an hour on the rocks after a shore lunch of fried pike and potatoes. Later, as we waited for the others to return from casting on the far side of X island, Ragnar and I chatted about the big Arctic grayling he had found for two brothers from Michigan on a recent day trip out of Yellowknife. The largest had topped 18 inches.

Late in the afternoon, the pike in Francois Bay went into a frenzy. For more than an hour, big fish were nailed cast after cast, shredding flies and leaders. The stories from Francois Bay were refined over beer at camp and will eventually mature into fine tales of triumph in the face of killer pike.

Sitting on the front step of the lodge after dinner, Dale and I watched the whitefish start their evening rise. We briefly discussed launching a canoe to fish the spinner fall, but in the end decided there had been a few too many beers consumed for safe boating.

On Sunday morning, when a light breeze lifted a lively chop around the islands, we retreated to sheltered bays along the mainland. After a little tenta-

Trout Rock Guide Frank Drygeese with one of Craig Cook's northern pike from the North Arm of Great Slave Lake.

tive action in Drygeese Bay, Frank took Greg and I into a series of coves named for Native trappers that once lived here. Jonas, Johnny and Dennis bays were alive with pike. When the Dogrib and Yellowknives were still widely dispersed on the land, there were cabins in most of the protected coves along the north shore. Frank smiled as he talked about travelling to Fort Rae by dog team past cabins with smoke curling up their chimneys. Those people are now only remembered by the names of the bays where once their cabins stood.

As we worked the weed beds, Frank taught Greg and I the Dogrib names for the fish in the North Arm: whitefish - li, northern pike - jhda, walleye - ehch'e, Arctic grayling - ts'et'ja, lake trout - liwezo and loche, prized for their livers, are - no'hkwe. While today you must travel closer to the main body of Great Slave Lake for trout and grayling, the rest of the species are all available around Trout Rock Island.

When we got down to trading recipes, Frank and I agreed that if we were going to eat fish everyday, we could do a lot worse than smoked whitefish. I had to admit, however,

that I really did not care for boiled fish. It is too bland.

My attention wandered as I chatted with Frank. I did not notice the telltale bulge in the surface before the strike, or when my line tightened and my reel started to scream. Shortly I was losing backing through my fingers. I recovered my line before the pike threw the hook but I never got it near the boat. All I saw as the line went limp was a streak of quicksilver headed for the bottom. As I gathered my line for the next cast, the Mega Diver drifted slowly back to the surface. A few minutes later, Greg landed a 44-inch pike with a girth of 19 inches. When Dale's boat slid alongside to view the release, he noticed an odd red tag on Greg's hook. "Oh that's a bit of plastic bread bag," Greg admitted", I forgot my orange flagging tape. You know the pike really seem to like that little bit of extra action behind the fly."

Later there was lively discussion over dinner about the fairness of red bread bag tail. It had, according to popular opinion, caused everyone else to have to reach into their pockets to pay off the pool. Greg quietly smiled as he slipped Frank a bit of the take.

Chapter Eight

Woodyard Jackfish—Urban Fishing in the Far North

Spring comes to Yellowknife in painfully slow fits and starts. Increasing solar heat drives the snow from all but the most sheltered nooks by late April. Five feet of ice locked in Great Slave Lake, however, keeps spring in suspended animation for another month. Through this periglacial period of blowing dust in the streets of Yellowknife, other hopeful signs keep one's attitude positive. The birch and aspen buds start to swell, but seldom burst before June. They offer a sign of hope that takes a long time to actualize. Spring, as I knew it as a boy in upstate New York, is generally less then a week long, as very late winter seemingly becomes summer.

By the latter part of April, there is enough open water in the Cameron River, 20 miles from town, to cast into a clear flow. Don't ask where the fish are at that time of year, for with my casting arm revived, the idea of a dead drift takes on a new meaning and I begin to look for any excuse to escape to Montana and fish the Yellowstone River. The near fishless water of April, however, gives way to renewed life in early May, as returning bald eagles perch along the open lower Yellowknife River to watch for the first movement of fish.

As the river's spring freshet pours under the edge of Great Slave Lake's winter coat, the remains of what must have once been great runs of pickerel and whitefish slide into the mouth. Those that hold in the pockets along the bedrock cliff on the west bank, can be sought with a gray or green weighted scud or small 1/32-ounce jigs dressed as olive and black woolly buggers. Persistence will often draw a strike. Despite the continued presence of the fish, they are but a shadow of the runs that formerly fed the Native Yellowknives that camped near the mouth of the river each spring.

Arctic Grayling once flowed up from Great Slave Lake, through Tartan Rapids and across Prosperous Lake to spawn in the Bluefish Riffles by the hydro-plant. My old Yellowknife neighbour Bob Bromley has boyhood memories of when the grayling seemed limitless. Today the run is a shadow of it's former self.

The city's other Arctic grayling fishery subsided years ago when they turned the Kam Lake system into a sewage lagoon. Miraculously, the northern pike, walleye and a few grayling survived and still run in small numbers each spring up into Grace Lake. Bob remembers walleye that were so thick the local kids tried to shoot them with 22 rifles. Now, despite improving water quality in Kam Lake, the flesh of the pickerel still has a chemical cocktail quality that is unfit to eat.

Today, serious Arctic grayling fishers must either fly far up the Yellowknife River system or wait until the ice clears among the islands of Great Slave Lake, between the Native community of Dettah and the headland at Gros Cap. The absence of Arctic grayling near town is once again testimony to their inability to

Bringing a northern pike to heal near Brabant Island on the Mackenzie River.

withstand fishing pressure and the deterioration of water conditions.

Grayling are not the only run that has faded before the growing city of Yellowknife. Prior to the MacMeekan causeway closing of the channel between the rock in "old town" and Latham Island, ciscos poured through the channel from Back Bay into Yellowknife Bay each spring. Disruption of that migration was another sign to the Native Yellowknives who used this fishery, that their traditional world had changed—perhaps forever. Before convenience stores, spring on the northern Canadian Shield could be a hungry time of year for Native families. Fish emerging from under the ice to spawn, were the first clear sign that their hunger would subside.

Since the city fathers of the old mining town of Yellowknife proudly completed their causeway in the 1950s, the continued growth of the city, now the capital of the Territories, has done more to complicate the Yellowknives' traditional lifestyle than simply fill a narrows. Traces of the early years of mining re-surfaced in the 1970s when high arsenic levels in fish from Back Bay made the Yellowknives' local subsistence fishery unusable. Recent tests by the Department of Indian Affairs and Northern Development, apparently indicate the fish are now edible, but as Yellowknife Chief Darrell Beaulieu notes, federal fishery officers have not rushed down to accept his invitation to a fish fry. As their hunting territories are turned into cottage country and the big lake bustles with boats it is hard not to share the lament of the Yellowknives over the impact of growth in this far northern city. Yellowknife has, with the transfer of civic responsibility north, become three levels of government sandwiched between two gold mines.

The Yellowknife waterfront shows the first signs of spring. Despite habitat loss from an encroaching marina, the Willow Flats below the "Woodyard" are still a wonderfully wild patch at the edge of Yellowknife's old town. Sometime in early May, the first shore leads appear along the grass flats below our old house. Shortly thereafter, the mallards, golden plovers and gulls appear. They are followed by a host of other shore birds. In the days that ensue, the flats collect waves of migrating song birds. As the ice slides out of the back channels and muskrat tracks, the northern pike slither in to spawn. Their arrival is announced by darting wakes and thrashing fish on the spawning beds. One day while stalking pike, I noticed the fresh green sprouts of the reborn reeds and was certain the season has changed.

Drifting between the flats and the ice edge in a canoe, I finally felt free from the grip of winter. Casting Hair Mice toward darting wakes, I anticipated the surge of the strike as I prepared to play the fish out away from the weeds. After each release, I shifted the rod and scanned the flats looking for long spurs or a muskrat. Pike taken on the surface were the first real dry "mouse" fish of the Yellowknife season. They are every bit as satisfying as the picky browns I had been casting Blue-Wing Olives to a few weeks earlier on a Montana spring creek. (Perhaps more so, for they were so much part of a place I know so well.)

Day by day as spring grew, the ice slipped further out until I could paddle to the houseboats by Jollife Island and have tea with friends. A few days later I would go out beyond the Dog Islands, to fish for trout that run past the seaward reach of the barren rocks in June. Working a streamer on a sinking line, I tried out new patterns that I would take further north later in the summer.

Carolyn Kobelka, a long time Woodyard resident, describes the narrow channel south of the "gut"

Willow Flats on the Yellowknife water front.

between the rock in old town and Joliffe Island as estuary-like. The feeling is right. Bound by the Dog Islands and Willow Flats, the narrows is an aquatic subset of Yellowknife Bay that has its own dynamics. From the tangle of tiny docks and old sunken wooden boats by "Buddies Beach" in the "Woodyard", to the earthen ramp of the Dettah ice road along School Draw, the half mile of flats were formed by the interplay of moving water. Though several miles from the mouth, there is a gentle flow that once moved through both Back and Yellowknife bays from the Yellowknife River. Still partially channeled through the "gut" it is one of the dynamics of the narrows. This influence is countered by the wind which pushes Great Slave Lake back up the bay. Protected by shoals, the narrows seldom get the heavier seas that roll up the centre of Yellowknife Bay.

Though the dynamics of the water flowing between the bays has been altered, and the habitat slowly eroded by foreshore development, Willow Flats has retained the core of its integrity. Behind Einar Broten's old blacksmith shop, the open grass reaches down to the water in a fairly even shoreline. The miners' shacks that once lined the slope between the meadow and Ragged Ass Road have slowly been replaced by fancy houses. Further south, the willows jut out to form a small headland. The flats then curve westward along a very shallow rocky bay next to School Draw Drive. While not as attractive to paddle, the far bay is alive with shorebirds. On an early spring day in the past, one could often find Jacques Sirois from the Canadian Wildlife Service there, busily working on his spring song bird count in the willows.

The tranquillity of spring along the flats is short lived. As soon as the drift ice has moved far enough down the bay that float planes can land safely on the water strip in the "gut", the hum of summer takes over. During the nightless days of June and July, the planes will buzz in and out nearly around the clock as geological camps, fishermen and fire crews are resupplied. Between the "gut" and Back Bay, there are over 5,000 float plane landings and takeoffs per year out of Yellowknife. By the time this happens, however, spring has moved further north.

After having missed a number of Yellowknife springs, I wandered back to the old neighbourhood with some trepidation. What would have happened to the flats in the last four years? As I strolled down the path by Grant Beck's old place, the only change seemed to be the movement of a culvert. The flats were, despite the lowest water levels in years, essentially unchanged. Beyond them, the bay has become busier as more brightly painted houseboats have sprouted in the lee of Joliffe and the Dog Islands. Remarkably, however, the ambiance has remained the same. The pike were slithering around in the spawning channels. Songbirds chimed in my ears as I inspected bursting willow buds. Later, when I went down to the Wild Cat Cafe for coffee, I ran into Bob and Marianne Bromley. When I mentioned my walk on the flats, Marianne bubbled with her first sighting of a Le Conte sparrow the day before. Lucy, the family's German Wirehair, had been out barking at the pike. It was obvious, despite continued threats, that the Willow Flats were as I remembered them. So few places stand the improvements of memory.

Chris Hanks with pike flies at Martin Lake near Yellowknife..

Chapter Nine

With Paddle and Rod

An aesthetic connection exists between the quiet parting of the waters by a cedar canoe and the gentle arc of a cane rod casting line to a distant rise. The actions of the two build toward the anticipated take of a native charr or grayling, whose ancestry is embedded in the water through which it swims. Union of the European fly rod and North American Indian birch bark canoe begin in the eastern waters of Maine, New Brunswick and Quebec's brook trout ponds and Atlantic salmon rivers. Once mated the pair found its way along the canoe routes and rail lines of the Canadian west. Early fly fishermen plied such storied waters as the Saint Mary's Rapids of Sault Ste. Marie, the Nipigon River for giant speckled trout called coasters and drew in Back's grayling from distant tributaries of Great Slave Lake.

Their mode of travel was the canoe. The canoe which slips through the water with the stroke of the paddle powered by the human arm. Arms that set the paddle across the gunwales, to pick up the rod and cast deceitful fur and feathers to fish whose ancestors arrived with the floods of departing glaciers. The fly rod easily joined the canoe to became part of the ancient cycle of life on the land in northern Canada.

Fly fishing has boomed in the later years of the 20th century. The sport has grown to provide tranquil hours on the water for those over stressed by urban life. In adopting fly fishing without the canoe, however, people are missing half the cure. Oh yes, I have heard the moans of those who proclaim the canoe tipsy and hard to use, but so can a fly rod be unwieldy in the hands of one who has not bothered to learn the rhythm of casting. Both are life skills that can be picked up at any age, the elements of which are learned in an afternoon, and then require the rest of your life to perfect. Besides, who in their right mind would not prefer to glide gracefully from shore, rather than have some small child do themselves harm laughing at your vain attempts to enter the water wearing your float tub, slapping flippers and flailing rod. More graceful is the art of winding a drift boat down a breaking current, but it lacks the canoes simplicity of design that has adapted it to the quiet flow and the raging torrent.

Let me make my bias clear, there is virtually no more perfect craft than the prospector canoe on a wild Canadian river. Built with healthy free board and an adequate rocker to twist and turn through the runs, haystacks and eddies of a rapids, it evolved into the workhorse of early geological exploration. For the recreational use, a 17-1/2-foot prospector will carry two people and their gear for three or four weeks a float. With camp set, one can quietly ply the shoal for rising fish and drift toward the nesting mallard's clutch. Perhaps I have already over played my hand in defense of the canoe as the ultimate Canadian Shield freedom machine, but come what may, it is true.

Across Canada and the United States there are many outdoor schools and weekend programmes run through organizations like the American Red Cross that will teach you how to paddle correctly. I learned in the Boy Scouts and while hunting moose with the Cree in northern Manitoba. Bill Mason's classic book, Path of the Paddle has been many peoples' first book on the sport. It is a good place to start.

If you decide you want to try canoe camping, see a lot of wildlife and do some fishing in the Territories, seriously consider a trip with an experienced outfitter. Alex Hall of Canoe Arctic Inc., out of Fort Smith, Black Feather Wilderness Adventures from Ottawa both take trips with the novice client in mind. To take advantage of some of the more advanced trips that provide the best fishing on the Barren Lands, you should plan to take some lessons from a local canoe club before you go and learn basic river skills.

Dismayed by the poor coverage the canoe gets in general fly fishing literature, from a press which trips over itself telling you how to improve the performance of your belly boat, I would like to offer a few suggestions for choosing and outfitting your canoe.

Once you have decided you want to buy a canoe, there are a number of decisions you have to make. Length, hull design and construction materials will all figure into your calculation. Try paddling as many hull designs as you can before you buy so that you make a choice that is right for you.

Today, AVS and Kevlar are the premium manmade materials most popular for back country canoe travel. There are some fine aluminum canoes made, but I find them to be too noisy as fishing crafts. For the purist who wants to go the extra mile, there are still lovely cedar and canvas, and cedar strip canoes made. I do not think there is anything more pleasing than paddling a cedar and canvas canoe. They are quiet, aesthetically in keeping with nature, and a wee bit heavy. If you are set on building your own canoe, the cedar strip boat is probably your best choice. Personally I have two fishing canoes—a 12-foot canvas and spruce Mountain Dene rat boat, and a 16-1/2-foot Kevlar Saugine. I use them for solo paddling and fishing. They were chosen for portaging weight and tracking when fishing alone. Neither is a boat I would choose to take on a Barren Land canoe trip, but then they

A tributary of the Kazan River near Snow Bird Lake.

Photo by John Gierach

were not bought for that purpose. If you are looking for a tough canoe that will bump and grind in the rapids, then an AVS craft is your best bet. When your back gets weary, you may want to consider a Kevlar boat.

There are a myriad of hull designs. As I mentioned before, the prospector with its mild rocker and high volume carrying capacity is a very good choice for most people. Although a lot has been written on the subject of canoe design, Ted Moores and Marilyn Mohr's Canoecraft is a good place to start. The book is about building wood strip canoes, but in the process they tell you a lot about the hull shape and design. The plans discuss the advantages of various style hulls, this information will assist you when you purchase your own canoe. Personally, I would stay away from flat bottom lake canoes. Although you may start canoeing on a small lake, being a fly fisherman, you will eventually want to move onto moving water. To do that you need at least a little rocker. The prospector and most other river canoes do not have a keel. When I bought my 16-1/2 footer to fish on lakes around Yellowknife, I selected a model with a slight keel that has proved a God send on windy Colorado mountain reservoirs. It helps the canoe track in crosswinds on lakes. For wilderness river travel, I use a boat without a keel.

There are a variety of canoe paddles available in a multitude of shapes. My favourites are: a long, narrow bladed cherry wood paddle for lake water, and a square laminated one for white water. Although my paddles are all wooden, there are some very functional plastic ones with aluminum shafts on the market.

After you have purchased a canoe, you may want to modify it by attaching Kevlar skid plates along the keel at the bow and stern. It is also a wise idea to install solid connections for your painters (bow and stern lines). The most important modification I make to my boats for solo fishing, however, is one I stole from solo white water paddlers. I install a six-inch-wide foam block between the centre thwart down the rear cargo hold to the stern thwart. This long slender piece of foam slides in tightly between the bottom of the canoe and the base of the thwart. It is easy to remove when you are not using it, but when you are out alone it provides an excellent paddling and casting position. Having bad knees, I find it makes kneeling in the boat all day much more comfortable. Unlike a float tub, where you can kick to maintain position while working your rod with your hands, a canoe sometimes requires an anchor. The classic canoe anchor drops from a small block at the bow or stern, allowing the boat to tether itself down the current. The block lets you handle the line from your sitting position in the canoe. Add-on anchor kits are available from many eastern sporting goods companies. Past the basics, you can glue foam blocks along the sides to hold hooks, add rod caddies, hang a mount over the side for a two horse gas engine or an electric trolling motor, and step a mast for a sail. In other words, you tailor it to your needs.

While my intent was not to convert fly fishermen to another sport, there is such a close link between the aesthetics of canoeing and fly fishing in northern waters that I felt compelled to leave a trail so that you could make your own link.

Chapter Ten

Big Lakes

The term Mackenzie Lowland is a bit deceiving. The reality is a world of big lakes and big rivers surrounded by ancient terraces, plateaus and tumbling tributaries that fall out of the Franklin and Mackenzie Mountains. Respectively, Great Bear Lake is the fourth and Great Slave Lake the fifth largest lake in North America. Did I almost forget to mention the Mackenzie River? It is the second longest river in North America. While on a map, the Mackenzie Lowlands may simply appear as the ground sandwiched between the Canadian Shield and the Mackenzie Mountains, it is in a very dynamic landscape full of many angling opportunities.

For the fly fisherman, the Mackenzie Lowlands hold the tributaries of the Mackenzie River drainage—a labyrinth of ancient highways that open a surprising country. If you have never considered fishing the Mackenzie River and its tributaries, think about it. It is no longer necessary to line canoes up tributaries to get to the headwater lakes. Float planes will whisk you inland over some extraordinary water to lodges. Interior lakes like Lac La Martre, Trout, Little Doctor, Kelly and Colville, provide a variety of flat water conditions and great insect hatches. Being forever a river fisherman, the brawling waters of the Kakisa, Trout, Blackwater, Keele, Great Bear, and Hare rivers have provided me with some wonderful fishing for Arctic grayling, northern pike, walleye, whitefish, Dolly Varden and bull

trout. There is a range of tributary water that runs from tiny streams where a seven-foot, 5 weight rod feels like a club to runs that can only be reached from a drifting boat.

While the Mackenzie River is not a white water experience, it is a unique corridor through the northern boreal forest that provides great angling. The river island shoals, big eddies and tributaries, have kept me busy for years and I have still only fished a few of them.

The streams of the Mackenzie Valley have carved their way down to the big river through sediments laid down at the close of the last ice age. The banks of the upper Mackenzie River are a layer cake of glacial lakes McConnell and Mackenzie. These sediments tell the story of the land since it emerged from under glacial ice. Before the Mackenzie cut through the limestone to form the Upper Ramparts, Lake Mackenzie drained over a falls to the west. The Fossil Creek channel across from Fort Good Hope provides access to the ancient plunge pool.

In many ways, the Mackenzie Valley is still recovering from the last ice age. One spring a few years ago, paleo-botanist Glen Macdonald and I collected pollen cores from lake bottoms to map the migration of jack pine down the Mackenzie Valley. In the 11,500 years since the ice retreated, jack pine have only migrated halfway down the Mackenzie Valley. Unlike spruce, jack pines require forest fires to crack open their cones so that their seeds can germinate. As a result, pines have been much slower to colonize the Mackenzie Valley than white and black spruce which nearly raced the glaciers north.

The Mackenzie Valley is a dynamic region that is distinctly different from the more "stately" bedrock landscape of the Precambrian shield on the east side of Great Slave and Great Bear lakes.

A Mackenzie Valley trip has many points of interest but some research is necessary to round out a full itinerary.

Below the Great Slave Lake outlet, the Mackenzie River flow is clear for many miles. The area around Big Island was used by the Hudson's Bay Company in the mid-19th century to produce provisions for its fur trade posts down the Mackenzie. Today, this rich environment is the home of Brabant Lodge. Located immediately south of Big Island, Brabant Island is situated in extremely fishy water.

There is a wonderful canyon full of falls on Big Smith Creek, south of Fort Norman. It is not a bad walk if you climb the north bank and follow the stream east along the edge of the muskegs. Do not follow my example though. Ron Yallee (from Fort Norman) and I, tried to walk up the streambed to the first falls. We finally gave up and raced the mosquitoes back to the Mackenzie River. Take the high ground, it is worth the trip. Did I mention that there were Arctic grayling above the canyon?

In June, when the water is high in the tributaries, there are float trips that start from one of the lakes that drain down to the Mackenzie River. They are a lot of fun. With canoes rented in Norman Wells strapped to the strut of North Wright Air's Plateaus Porter, it is only a short flight across the Franklin Mountains, into Kelly Lake on the Brackett River. The lakes and rivers along the Brackett system have great northern pike fishing. From Kelly Lake, the river winds downstream past the Dene hunting camp above Willow Lake (Brackett Lake on the topographic map). The lake is a major stopover on the Mackenzie flyway. During the spring and fall, migration rafts of geese and swans seem to cover the lake. How do you describe the ornithological experience of a lifetime? After watching the swans and chasing a few pike, it is an easy paddle down the Brackett River to the Great Bear River. Arctic grayling hold in the Great Bear a short distance above the mouth of the Brackett River. From the mouth of the Great Bear River at Fort Norman, it is a 50-mile paddle down the Mackenzie River to Norman Wells. What a very pleasant way to spend a couple of weeks.

During July and August, Dene fish camps still dot the banks of the Mackenzie along the big eddies of the Upper Ramparts, above Fort Good Hope. Once fish camps lined the river from Fort Providence to Aklavik, now they grace only a few sections of the river where the old people still return each year to fish.

I know the map calls many of the tributaries of the Mackenzie River, rivers, but I have always agreed with my old travelling companion, George Barnaby, who believes that after the Mackenzie, nothing else seems like a river.

Despite my optimism, the Lowlands can be a hard place to fish. It is not easy to get into many of the interior lakes. Much of the best fishing occurs right after the ice goes out or during spawning runs. It takes local knowledge to be there at the right time. The easiest way is to go through a guiding service or one of the lodges.

The only lodge on the Mackenzie River is Brabant Island, located below the outlet of Great Slave Lake. Brabant Island Lodge focuses on northern pike, Arctic grayling, walleye and whitefish in the clear headwaters of the Mackenzie River.

Two of the more interesting establishments on interior lakes are Meni Dene Lodge on Lac La Martre a half hour flight northwest of Yellowknife and Colville Lake Lodge an hour by air northeast of Norman Wells. Both facilities offer superb fishing for lake trout, Arctic grayling, northern pike and whitefish. Additionally, Colville Lake presents the possibility of inconnu—a large cousin of the whitefish that is known in Alaska as sheefish. The inconnu is a voracious predator and an infamous, if somewhat unknown, fighter. When the inconnu make false spawning runs into the creeks, they can be taken on a fly rod with streamers.

If walleye are on your mind, then Trout Lake Lodge during the spring run in June is for you. Located 45 minutes southeast of Fort Simpson by air, it provides one of the best walleye fisheries in the NWT.

If fishing the west side of Great Bear Lake strikes your fancy, Morris Modeste from Deline normally guides on Keith Arm and Great Bear River. He will, if given enough lead time, take people to the Johnny Hoe River for walleye in the spring too. Great Bear River is a place I return to fish every chance I get. Drifting the rapids for Arctic grayling when the grasshoppers are on is like having the Yellowstone River to yourself. To the east, Plummer's Lodge operates five lodges on the lake that offer a variety of fishing options. The choice is between being alone with Morris in tent camps, or having the comforts of big lodges. Either way, you will have good fishing.

Catching lunch of a creek of Great Bear Lake.

Chapter Eleven

Pickerel Road—Fishing Near The Mackenzie Highway

Three days out of Vancouver and six hours north of Manning, Alberta the numbness in my spine raised the question that the vertebra were fusing. The truck's lack of pretensions made the paved roads in northern Alberta feel like an abandoned logging track. I could hardly wait for the gravel north of the border. A Spartan 4 wheel drive's virtues lay off the beaten track once one has arrived in the outback, getting there is another matter.

Droning tires filled the dead air as the last local radio station, in High Level, Alberta, faded into the distance. Passing the tiny settlement of Indian Cabins, I mused about fishing in the Territories. I was ready to break the trip, go for a hike, and try out the new graphite fly rod that my wife's cousin had given me. Reaching the border promised new water and Arctic grayling, a species that had intrigued me since boyhood.

Although I did not expect much insight from the docents at the information kiosk on the NWT/Alberta border, I was crestfallen when they smiled and reiterated together "... you want to fly fish?" They allowed as how you could take Arctic grayling on a fly, but I would have to go further north. I was dismayed by their ambivalence toward fishing near the highway between the border and Yellowknife. Had I entered the north, the land of fish, with over inflated expectations or was I simply lacking essential information about my next step? I pondered the question as I watched the Hay

River plunge over Alexander Falls. Flowing water lulled my weariness as the excitement of having arrived re-inflated my curiosity. What did the folks at an information stand really know? It was obvious I simply had to find the fish by myself. That 24th of May weekend was the start of exploring for fish near the NWT highway system.

Possessed by the grip of the road, I passed on an excursion off the main highway, to the community of Hay River on that first trip. If I had taken the time and asked a few questions, I might have found some fish and it would certainly have given me an opportunity to relieve the pain in my back.

The town of Hay River is the terminus of the railroad, and the head of navigation on the Mackenzie River. Tugs and barges line the banks. Starting in late June, it is the kickoff point for fishermen headed to Brabant Lodge in the Mackenzie River. The lodge is famous for northern pike, Arctic grayling, whitefish, walleye and hospitality. While fishing in the lower Hay River is not the wilderness experience you will find at Brabant, it is surely a northern one that does produce walleye.

Later, I explored the lower Hay River by canoe. Camping at the government campground on Vale Island in Hay River's old town, I got a feel for life on the river as barges bound for the communities on Great Slave Lake and the Mackenzie River chugged in and out. It is a big water that requires attention to commercial traffic and local knowledge to really appreciate its fishing potential. On my first trip, I concluded that reading the brown water meant looking for other fishermen. I was rewarded by several gentle tugs from walleye and the odd squeal of a northern pike stripping line from my reel. I must admit, however, I was puzzled at how to take walleye consistently on the fly.

The walleye come into the river from Great Slave Lake in early July and remain until September. A 14- to 16-foot aluminum boat or canoe will handle the river, but you must remember that until you get above the Northern Transportation Company (NTCL) docks, you are in a busy shipping lane. Barges and tugs can not maneuver around a poorly handled small craft. Above the docks, the river is shallow and requires care to avoid banging your propeller.

Recently, when I stopped to visit Dale Freschi on my way back from Brabant Lodge, he could hardly wait to get me out on the river. A few days earlier, he had finally broken the walleye fly riddle. He and a friend had had a 30 fish evening on the fly, within the city limits of Hay River.

For a long time, fishing for walleye on the fly has been problematic for me. Occasionally I took fish, but I was not getting consistent results. In fact, as recently as the day before that evening with Dale, John Propp (a Spokane fly shop owner) and I had sat on the deck at the lodge speculating on how to consistently take more walleye on the fly. At that sitting, we figured that the Clouser Minnow held promise, but neither of us had had impressive enough results to backup our considered opinions.

While we theorized, Dale was out discovering that walleye can be consistently taken on flies with large Muddler Minnow heads. The secret is to displace a lot of water. The heavily weighted fly is worked right along the bottom. Commercially they have names like "fat head minnow" or "Mega Diver". Touted in fly shops as surface lures for northern pike, the smaller ones double nicely as walleye menaces when they are sunk to the bottom. The most successful pattern is in fact, simply a large tufted hair head that is between 3/4 to one inch long, and 1/2 to 3/4 of an inch wide at the back. Ours were tied on long shank size 2 hooks. Behind the fat head there is a sparse, short deer hair tail mixed with Krystal Flash. The tail extends 1/2 inch behind the iron. If it is too long, shorten it. Though this sounds prescriptive, there seems to be a very fine balance between having a large head which displaces a lot of water and one that interferes with hooking one-and-1/2 to two-pound walleye. Walleye that strike a fly are often lost at the set. The very thin tail that shrouds the hook seems to provide better hookups than a thicker bodied streamer. We further improved our hooking ratio on the Hay River by removing the weed guards from the flies. An apt name for the fly is simply "head and tail".

Natural deer hair heads with painted eyes have proved very effective in the muddy waters of the Hay River. When the natural hair variants start to fall off, bright green, black and dark red flies have all turned the trick. The choice of colour is more critical in clearer waters where visibility is better. On the Hay River the disturbance caused by the fly seems more important then the actual colour. A well stocked walleye fly box should also include weighted Woolly Buggers, 1/32-ounce jig heads with Woolly Bugger bodies, Clouser Minnows, Zonkers and a medley of streamers you would use for northern pike and big trout.

The size of the flies and the fish in the Hay River, lend themselves to a stiff 6 or 7 weight rod. Although a sinking tip works, a full sinking line with a short tippet is ideal.

Dale was disappointed the night he took me out to showoff his discovery, we only took 15 or 16 fish. Be that as it may, we out-fished the hardware crowd around us. He was jubilant that he was able to make his breakthrough in time for me to include it in this book.

Embarrassingly, rubber worms fished with gentle twitches on a fly rod are even better than muddlers. They outperform the same lure on a spinning rod and provide a very effective search pattern for walleye on big water. Find the fish and switch back to a hand tied fly. (Anglers do lure swordfish up with bait and blood before casting to them with a streamers.) As Dale shyly points out every sport has its black side but if it helps to find the walleye and prevents a skunking then it's worth a try. Finding fish in big water sometimes requires candy and walleye simply love gently twitched rubber worms.

When I fished the Hay River with Dale, we concentrated on the bend in the main channel between Vale Island and the Hay River reservation. If you are uncertain, contact a guide who knows the river. This is particularly wise if you are not used to sharing the water with commercial navigation.

By the time I saw the sign for Lady Evelyn Falls on the Kakisa River during my inaugural trip, I was down to searching for road signs for hooked fish below campground designations. In reality, if simply looking at the Kakisa River in spring does not trigger your fish reaction, then you do not deserve to catch any. The fishermen below the falls on that first trip mentioned Arctic grayling, but were intently catching northern pike that follow the spawning grayling and walleye up the Kakisa River each spring. The grayling are what make the river famous, but the walleye are worth finding. I missed the grayling and walleye that day, but later took my first northern pike on a fly in the NWT, several miles below the falls.

The Kakisa River is big by fly fishing standards—it is more then a 100 yards wide, averaging depths of three to five or more feet in the main channel at normal flows. I honestly do not know how deep the plunge pool is below the migratory barrier at Lady Evelyn Falls. One can, however, wade substantial portions of the river below it in chest-high waders.

After the ice in the river clears, the water level and temperature is controlled by the melting ice in Kakisa Lake. At night, the thaw slows. By morning the river has fallen, warmed and cleared. As the morning sun nibbles at the ice, the process reverses and by mid-afternoon, on warm days in May, the water level at the Mackenzie Highway bridge is rising, the temperature drops and the flow goes slightly off colour.

On the Kakisa River, Arctic grayling, northern pike, and walleye all run following breakup. Depending upon how badly I want to hang onto a big pike if I hook one, I occasionally set aside my 5 or 6 weight for an 8 weight that can hold a big pike.

Years after that initial trip, I introduced myself to Dale in the same riffle I had taken the pike. He was teaching his sons the ethics of catch and release Arctic grayling angling. Since the grayling were devastated by disease in the late 1980s, the fishery is now restricted to catch and release. Under this enlightened management regime, the Arctic grayling are coming back. The run starts in late April, as soon as the fish can breakout from beneath the ice in the Mackenzie River and scoot up the Kakisa. Early in the run, the grayling are taken on Stonefly Nymphs drifted along the bottom. In late May, there is a spectacular black stonefly hatch shortly before the fish drop back into the big river. A slender 2X, size 8 or 10 dry pattern seems to be the right size for the hatch. There were stoneflies hatching as Dale and I fished, but the grayling had not started to rise yet.

Out of deference to their relatively small mouths, I generally stop at a size 8 nymph when fishing for grayling. Dale however, was very successfully using a size 2 Stonefly Nymph. With a smile he noted that the larger hook helped select the bigger fish out of the run. The winning pattern that day was Joe Brooks' Montana Stonefly tied in the round so that it flared its hackle as it tumbled along the bottom. Responding to the size, and speed, of the Kakisa River I was using a high density line with a short leader and a weighted fly to keep my nymph on the bottom. I found however, that I was not doing nearly as well with it as Dale was by using a floating line with a long leader and a strike indicator. He relied simply on a heavily weighted fly to take his tippet to the bottom. It was a system designed to telegraph the gentle tug of a grayling to the surface.

On my earlier visits to the Kakisa River, I was out-fished by anglers using spinning tackle. The fast, deep water favored the lower drag of spinning line and the concentrated weight of a metal lure that sank quickly to the bottom. Initially, I experimented with sinking tip lines. I quickly abandoned them, however, in favor of a high density full sinking line. As a result of those experiences, until I was out-fished by Dale and his floating line, I pretty much followed Joe Brooks' method for nymphing big flows. If the current was really heavy, I attached a small lead head, and loaded more split shot on the short leader. The object was to get the terminal tackle onto the bottom and let the fly bounce up into the current just off the rocks where the fish were feeding. Although Dale may not have had his fly as firmly on the bottom as I did, his approach works better however, in light of the way the grayling strike. My strategy was not delicate angling, but after a long subarctic winter it was fly fishing. Dale was having more fun.

Kakisa Lake lies several miles above the falls. The access road to Kakisa village stops by its shore. The most consistent pickerel fishing is along a drop-off at the inflow of the Kakisa River across the lake. When Carolyn Kobelka and I paddled Kakisa Lake, we found a "classic" boreal forest impoundment. Ancient beach ridges spread from the gravel shore up through the willows and into a black spruce forest. Freshwater mussel shells littered the gravel. The shallow shoreline of glacial till and lake sediments along the southeast shore pushed powered skiffs out toward the centre of the lake until a thumb of deep water allowed them to turn back into the mouth of the river. The drop-off in the lake, off the inflow of the river, is the focus of the commercial fishery run by the Native Slavey who live near Kakisa Lake. It is also a wonderful opportunity to fish with a sinking line on a 6 or 7 weight rod after the ice goes out in the spring. Regrettably, when the pickerel fishery is at its best, the bugs are at their worst. Fishing south of Great Slave Lake in the spring is always a balance between fabulous fish runs and your tolerance for mosquitoes.

The Mackenzie River ferry crossing above Fort Providence provides an opportunity to launch your boat on the big river. Hiring a guide with local knowledge will greatly improve your chance of success with the northern pike, grayling and whitefish found in the upper river. The Mackenzie is a large, often swift flow that requires more than novice boating skills when conditions are less than perfect.

Fort Providence also provides the closest dependable motel accommodations to the Kakisa River.

North of Fort Providence, the Mackenzie Highway swings inland through the Mackenzie Wood Bison Sanctuary. Fifteen years ago, you seldom, if ever, saw the great shaggy wood bison. Now it is rare not to see them. Years ago, a small number of pure wood bison were planted east of the highway at Falaise Lake. Over the years, spottings along the highway have become more common as the herd has grown. Recently, on my way to the Kakisa River, I photographed a solitary old bull sleeping at the edge of Fort Providence. Early in the morning a few days later, I saw two herds, one of young bulls, the other a nursery

group of protective mothers and their fluffy, cinnamon-coloured calves. The young were still bedded down along the edge of the trees as their nervous mothers eyed the road. The return of the wood bison north of the Mackenzie River is a step toward re-populating their historic range in the upper Mackenzie Valley and a boon to the visitor.

Since my first drive, the change in the road has been miraculous. The Mackenzie Highway is now largely paved between Fort Providence and the turnoff to Fort Rae, turning it into a pleasant drive through the boreal forest. When we moved to Yellowknife in the early 1980s, the highway felt like an overgrown jeep track frequented by 18-wheelers plunging through clouds of dust. As I cruised at 70 mph, I marveled at the smooth ride and wondered when they would pave the rest of the road to Yellowknife.

Remembering back, I can still feel the slow paralysis that crept up my spine from the unforgiving suspension of the truck. Just as it had reached unbearable proportions, I broke out of the forest. Before me sprawled the North Arm of Great Slave Lake. A few minutes later, as I bumped across a creek culvert, I caught sight of fishermen standing arm to arm in the water below. My travel weary mind registered fish as I swung into the North Arm Campground. The place was a madhouse of screaming kids and campers packed cheek to jowl. Waiting in line at the outhouse, I played tourist and asked what they were fishing for. "Pickerel," the guy in front of me exclaimed, "best run of the year". The Mosquito Creek walleye run was, in those years, an annual rite of spring that transformed tranquil northern waters into mayhem. After a walk to the creek, and a quick look around the campground, I decided this was not for me. Fortunately for the walleye that were trying to spawn, the Department of Fisheries and Oceans decided they did not much care for the debauchery either and closed the run in the late 1980s. Mosquito Creek is now secured against anglers from May 1st to July 1st. It generally re-opens just in time for the whitefish run. Although scoffed at by hardware fishermen as uncatchable, fly fishermen often do well with these difficult prey. The real reward comes when you eat them and discover why many northerners prefer whitefish to other species for the table.

Deprived of easy pickins', some anglers started to make the longer journey into Dory Creek, on the far side of Marian Lake, across from the community of Fort Rae. Dory's isolation, beyond the mud flats on the far side of the lake, has saved it from becoming the debacle that Mosquito Creek degenerated into.

For those not inclined to cope with the shallow, often windy waters of Marian Lake, and the mud flats at the creek mouth, the west channel culvert on the Mackenzie Highway by the community of Edzo, offers a shot at migrating walleye.

Fortunately, nothing matches the scene at Mosquito Creek. With the pressure off, that run is now making a comeback. The harvest of spawning walleye on the North Arm touches the fishery on all of Great Slave Lake. North Douglas, a Métis friend from Edzo, told me he has seen walleye with fisheries tags from Gros Cap, on the East Arm, Hay River and Fort Resolution, on the south shore of the lake, come out of Dory Creek. Harm that run and you impact the walleye

fishery on the fifth largest freshwater lake in North America.

For a long time, Dory Creek was one of those dates on my fishing calendar that never happened. When I returned north last spring, Gordon Lennie and North Douglas asked me to go along. The fishing during the last weekend in May had been spectacular. How could I refuse a trip to the source? I found some 1/32-ounce and 1/8-ounce jigs at the discount store, picked up some model paint, and dug out my Black and Yellow Marabou. I wanted jigs that would not overpower my 6 weight rod. We were a little late. The peak flow of fish up the creek had been a week earlier but what the heck, there would still be walleye that, with luck, would grace my line.

An early start in June is 10 o'clock. The days are long and warm. When Gordon and I arrived in Edzo, we found North laid out on the side deck drinking coffee and enjoying a smoke. He yawned, "You caught me. I was about to go to Fort Rae for gas." Off he went as his wife plied us with eggs and sausage. A pot of coffee later, North reappeared to haul us to the boat. At the west channel landing we were confronted with an empty river bank. "Where's the damn boat?" North muttered some curse about the local kids and sent me back for his canoe and little kicker. As Gordon and I settled down for a chat, North and his sidekick Hugh McSwain disappeared around the bend. When the motor faded we assumed they had found the boat. Hours later, however, they returned from the opposite direction. Minutes after leaving us, the four horse had seized. (North had recently loaned it to someone who must have run it without oil mix.) They spent the next three hours poling through backwaters looking for the big aluminum skiff. When they found it, they had to paddle both boats back. As we finally pulled from shore, I noticed that it was five o'clock.

With historically low water on Marian Lake, it was necessary to pole across flats that one normally skims over at speed. To get into Dory Creek, Hugh and North finally had to jump out and drag us across the bar. Passing over deep holes in the lower creek, scores of walleye hung below us as we headed for the first rapids. Dory Creek has cut its bed down through old glacial lake sediments, leaving relatively steep banks with fine undercuts. The lower stream comes gently down through a series of big pockets, deep runs and riffles that can be comfortably navigated with a small boat and motor or a canoe. Crossing the shallow, often choppy waters of Marian Lake, however, a shallow draft boat with adequate free board is more comfortable than a canoe.

Below the rapids, North stationed himself on a small point by a deep pocket. He was quickly into a fish. The rest of us staggered ourselves up to the base of the rapids. It was obvious watching North that he was feeling his jig as he worked it across the bottom. His line hand, sensitive to the slightest nudge of a take, was quick to set the hook. The man is a real pickerel fisherman.

I worked a sinking tip line down and across a deep pocket at the base of the rapids. I hoped my yellow and white palmered jig looked like a fleeing bait fish as it gently bounced across the bottom. On the third cast, I felt a gentle tug and missed the set. Eventually, as we worked downstream, I missed three more strikes before I tied into a nice fish. As I

brought it to the surface, it shook violently and broke free. When I retrieved the jig, I found the hook had broken at the bend.

Dory Creek was past the wild frenzy of catch and release that had characterized the water a week earlier. The fish were well fed and lethargic after feeding on fry moving downstream. Though catching was no longer easy, even for old masters like North, our efforts were successful in drawing the odd strike and producing enough fish for dinner. With a few fish in the boat, we left Dory Creek and headed for the Marian Lake fire tower to spend the night with North's father Bob Douglas.

After circling the lake for hours looking for ducks, we finally arrived at the base of the mountain at 11 o'clock at night. North would have liked to have called it a traditional Native spring hunt, but he never got close enough to a raft of black ducks to connect.

Thank God for the Arctic summer. Where else could you start a 1,000-foot climb in the middle of the night? Despite a growing weariness, the hike was a wonderful walk up great exposures of bedrock, ancient beach ridges, and finally the crags in the rock band below the summit. My legs got stronger as I went until, by the time I reached the top, I was wide awake and totally invigorated. When Hugh and I walked into the cabin, Bob peeked out of his sleeping bag and mumbled, "I thought I was going to have to call out the dogs to find you guys."

By the time Gordon and North sauntered in, Bob was up making tea. North reached into his pack and pulled out a fine bottle of Irish whisky that a friend had picked up for Bob at the duty free in Shannon. Turning it in his hand Bob mused, "I have not had this since the old squadron broke up in 45." Glasses clinked and somehow the cap for the bottle was lost. In the wee hours, I vaguely remember North commenting on how smoothly the elixir slid down.

Gordon, Bob and I slid out fairly early the next morning and sat out on the tower deck, drinking coffee and looking down over Marian Lake. It was a beautiful summer day, slightly tinged with the smoke of distant forest fires. North and Hugh had had a long day yesterday chasing boats and ducks. As they snoozed on through the morning, we reflected on Hugh's promise to make us pancakes last night. Nibbling on toast, Bob told us about walking several hundred miles to the Barren Lands with the Dogribs from Fort Rae for the fall caribou hunt when he was a young wildlife officer. He spoke of reading old messages from near-mythic bush pilots at a cairn by the ruins of Fort Enterprise on Winter Lake. The fort had been the winter quarters of the ill-fated first Franklin expedition in 1821 and 1822. The British sailors had struggled back to the fort from the Arctic coast hungry, nearly broken men, who would surely have perished if a party of Native Yellowknives had not come north from "Old Fort Providence", near modern Yellowknife, to relieve them. Like John Franklin's men, Bob had arrived by canoe with a Native hunting party. The similarities of circumstance and a strong sense of place had had a lasting impression on him.

After a big feed of walleye and a low-key day reflecting on the people and places in the Mackenzie who's acquaintance Bob and I shared, it was time to go.

At the boat, North rubbed his hands, and mused, "Ducks anyone?" An hour later I was beginning to feel like the little kid who complained to his mother that he was tired of running in circles. She retorted, "Be quiet Johnny or I will nail your other shoe to the floor." Another flight of ducks circled and around we went again. Eventually a lack of cigarettes forced the guys to head for the convenience store in Fort Rae. Re-supplied we started down the west channel to Edzo, coffee, and the road to Yellowknife. Gordon dropped me off at midnight after a wonderful weekend of walleye and memories of another fishery off the Mackenzie Highway. The docents were wrong you know.

Lady Evelyn Falls on the Kakisa River.

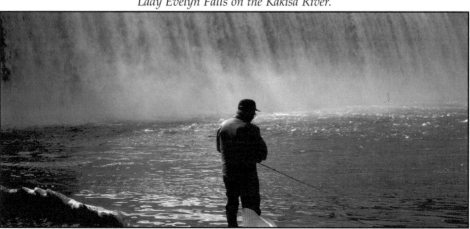

Chapter Twelve

Two Faces Of The Mackenzie River

The Mackenzie River provides a variety of angling opportunities along its 1,089 mile course. Between Great Slave Lake and the village of Tuktoyaktuk on the Arctic Ocean the river moves through North America's most northerly forest. North of the community of Fort Good Hope it crosses the Arctic Circle. It is a formidable body of water, varying from six miles near the outlet to a mere 1/2 mile in the confines of the upper Ramparts. When its major tributary, the Liard River floods, the Mackenzie can be choked with logs. A strong north wind ripping against its current will throw up three- to four-foot waves. When that happens, you pull the boat in and sit on the bank around a fire. On a calm summer's day, however, the Mackenzie benignly tumbles along at 4 to 6 knots. The hours slip by as the river slowly descends through an everchanging subarctic landscape. Despite its size, the Mackenzie River has only two real sets of rapids—the Sans Sault by the mouth of the Mountain River and the Upper Ramparts. Both are navigable by small boats that follow the shipping channel without having to run "white water".

Unlike many places in the Northwest Territories, there is road access to the Mackenzie River. Hay River off the Mackenzie Highway, is the first access point on the way north from Edmonton. Situated on the south shore of Great Slave Lake, it is the first launching point for large boats. Hay River is also the point of departure for the short flight to Brabant Lodge on the Mackenzie River. Further west, the Fort Providence ferry crossing and Fort Simpson provide opportunities to launch boats on the Mackenzie River and meet local guides. Fort Simpson is also the hub for air access to Nahanni National Park in the southern Mackenzie Mountains. On the backside of the Mackenzie Highway loop, Blackstone Park Territorial Park, south of Fort Simpson on the Liard Highway, provides camping and a boat launch on the Liard River on the way to the Alaska Highway. Following the new extension of the Mackenzie Highway west, you can drive on from Fort Simpson to the Camsell Bend ferry and continue north to the small Native community of Wrigley in the central Mackenzie Valley. When Alexander Mackenzie first descended the river, now named after him, in 1789, he thought it might flow west to the Pacific. When the river turned north at Camsell Bend he is thought to have named it the "river of despair". Fishermen need not feel his apprehension, the Mackenzie River provides a world of opportunity.

Daily jet service from Edmonton and Yellowknife to Norman Wells can link with local air carriers to provide access to outfitters in Fort Norman, Norman Wells and Fort Good Hope, along the central Mackenzie River. Connections can also be made to Deline, on Great Bear Lake.

The Dempster Highway through the Yukon Territory provides road access to the Mackenzie delta communities of Fort MacPherson on the Peel

River, and Arctic Red River and Inuvik on the Mackenzie River. There are numerous local guide services out of these communities.

While the clear water section of the Mackenzie River between the outlet of Great Slave Lake and the lower end of Beaver Lake is the best known to fly fishermen, good fishing can also be found along other sections of the river with a little scouting. Generally, anglers encounter a mix of Arctic grayling and northern pike; but walleye, Dolly Varden or bull trout, lake trout, sheefish or inconnu and whitefish are also present. Under the right circumstances, all of these fish can be taken on a fly rod. Lake whitefish, which feed on scuds most of the time, often rise for mayflies and caddis. Northern pike will respond either to surface or subsurface tactics, but are most readily taken with a sinking pattern. Walleyes and sheefish are sought almost exclusively with streamers and sinking lines. Although chum salmon run up the Mackenzie River across Great Slave Lake to the Slave River, they have stopped feeding and changed colour by the time they reach the upper drainage in late fall. Dene and Inuit elders occasionally speak of taking bright salmon near the Beaufort Sea but I have never been able to track the Mackenzie delta salmon streams down. I suspect it is the type of secret that a Native fisherman would rather take to his grave than tell a fishing writer.

Conventional wisdom states that Arctic grayling avoid the turbid river below Fort Simpson, where the silt load of the Mackenzie River is multiplied by the tumultuous waters of the Liard River. While it is true that the best Arctic grayling fishing is in the clear water of the upper 1/3 of the Mackenzie River, opportunities do exist below Fort Simpson. The lower Mackenzie River is a highway to the tributaries.

My introduction to blue fish, as the Native Slavey refer to Arctic grayling, was around the mouths of tributaries on the lower river. During my first summer on the Mackenzie River in 1982, John Shae and George Barnaby from Fort Good Hope, took me to Fish Creek above the spectacular Upper Ramparts Canyon on the Mackenzie River. The low water levels of late summer had left the creek but a modest trickle. This served our purposes to a tee; we were there looking for the remains of stonefish weirs that Slavey people would have used to trap grayling during their spawning run.

Despite the promise of spring, the end of winter was traditionally a hungry time of the year. The Mackenzie River was busy breaking up five feet of winter ice, the inland lakes were covered with slush and the thawing muskegs made overland travel difficult. By placing his family near the mouth of an Arctic grayling creek in late winter, a hunter could use the fish that flowed upstream into the clear water to help break his family's hunger in early spring. The grayling provided a welcome relief to the dwindling store of dried meat that might include snowshoe laces, if it had been a particularly hard winter.

Traces of the weirs and the camps that accompanied them have been removed by countless spring freshets. The role of Arctic grayling in the traditional Native use of the Mackenzie River fishery is so vividly recorded in oral traditions, that one can almost smell their delicate flesh roasting on hot rocks, amid a spring hunting camp full of screaming children and barking dogs. The opening of the creeks and arrival of the grayling signaled the start of the spring hunt when roast beaver and muskrat would soon become camp staples. It was a time of reunion for families after a long winter when they were separated in small outposts along the Mackenzie Valley.

Being a seasonally sensitive fisherman, I should have been thinking about whitefish and inconnu or connie instead of Arctic grayling at that time of the year on the lower Mackenzie River. The problem was that in the early 1980s very few people considered whitefish, let alone connie, as a fly rod species. My Slavey companions fished for them with gill nets. A couple of years later, my friend Tom Andrews was casting off a little creek across the Mackenzie River from Fish Creek. It was an August day, when the inconnu made a false spawning run. These carnivorous cousins of the whitefish average 18 to 30 inches. A school was chasing bait fish in the creek mouth where Tom was fishing. For the half of an hour or so that the connie were in, Tom had wild action. Then as suddenly as they appeared, the inconnu were gone. The connie are favoured by the Slavey for smoking. In the late summer, the banks of the Mackenzie were once lined with Native fish camps with teepees full of smoking inconnu and whitefish. I will still stack smoked connie against salmon.

Several years later I had the chance to try fishing the spring Arctic grayling run on a small creek along the Dempster Highway, south of Inuvik. The flood of the Mackenzie River made the lower creek so murky that the fish could not see the Partridge and Orange I drifted before their noses. Despite my frustration I marked their

passage by counting the long delicate dorsal fins that broke the surface as the grayling swam up into the culvert under the highway. I thought about following them to the clear water, but was discouraged by a black bear sow and her cub poking along in the willows on the other side of the highway. If I ever had any doubt that Arctic grayling lived in the murky lower Mackenzie River that evening cured it.

My dry spell was broken on that trip when I stopped off in Fort Good Hope on the way back to Yellowknife for a meeting. After we were all talked out, I took a couple of nice northern pike out of Jackfish Creek right behind the community on a Black and Yellow Sneaky Pete. The fly is simple. It is merely a reversed cork popper head followed by lots of marabou. Because it is a quick fly to tie it is a good substitute for Dahlberg Divers, which are more easily destroyed by pike. When retrieved with a jerking motion my rendition of a Sneaky Pete dives nicely. Slack the line and it races for the surface. All in all the erratic motion is a satisfactory response for a small critter in shallow water infested with big northerns. The fish agreed.

The creek mouths and eddies along the Mackenzie River present good opportunities to pursue northern pike. Pike fishing near Fort Good Hope is very good too.

My Arctic grayling education really got started the year after Fish Creek, when I actually caught a grayling on the Mackenzie River. George Pellissey and I were weathered-in south of Fort Norman, at the mouth of the Blackwater River. When it became obvious that the wind that had driven us off the Mackenzie River was not going to subside, over a pot of coffee George suggested that we go grayling fishing.

George threw me his spinning rod and said, "Flick the spinner over there." I thought I hit the mark but the empty wiggling spinner confirmed my miss. Impatiently, George took the rod back and immediately hooked a fish. Although I began to catch on, George still out-fished me by three to one. With dinner in hand, we headed back to camp intent on giving everyone a break from canned stew. My offer to clean the fish was met with a curious, "Why?".

George dragged me off to collect armloads of green willow switches. Back in camp, his wife Vivian built the fire up and let it die down repeatedly until she had a rich bed of coals. Upon our return with a huge plastic tarp full of willows, George piled a big arm load of them on the coals and threw a half dozen whole fish on top. As the smoke began to curl up through the thick bed of bows, George regularly turned the fish so that they would cook gently and not burst any internal organs. When the pile of willow began to settle into the charcoal, and the blackened scales lifted from the steaming flesh, the fish were pronounced cooked. Served on fresh spruce bows, the hot scales were gingerly lifted back and the white flesh gingerly picked out with our fingers. Accompanied by quantities of strong bush tea and fresh fried bannock, no finer meal could have been found along the Mackenzie River.

That night, after all the fish remains had been carefully put back in the river, and the greasy spruce thrown far into the bush, I had my first lesson on grizzly bears. When I awoke in the morning and unzipped the front of my tent, I was confronted by a bear track two hands wide, six inches from where my head had been. The camp was clean and so all brother bear had found were interesting smells, and perhaps the odd sound of our nylon tents flapping in the breeze. Generally speaking there are not grizzlies in the Mackenzie Valley, but in recent years a few have come down the new winter road from Great Bear Lake. The Blackwater River valley seems to be particularly to their liking.

After my experience at Fish Creek, I assumed that by late August, when George and I would be at the Blackwater River, that there would not be many Arctic grayling around the tributary mouths of the Mackenzie River. The grayling spawn in the spring. During the summer, I had been told, they hung around the head end of islands. While that is true, it is not the whole story. On some of the larger swift tributaries that maintain cooler summer temperatures, the grayling stay around the mouth moving out into the plume of freshwater to feed along the current line between the flow from the tributary, and the brown of the silt laden Mackenzie River.

A few days later, at the mouth of Saline Creek, George began to teach me a few tricks about big river eddies. The Saline drainage is choice Dene hunting territory. Salt licks upstream draw moose down the valley from the lower slopes of the Franklin Range, while the salinity of the creek seems to add a little flair to the fishery in Mackenzie River below the confluence. George equivocated, then mused, "I know it is illegal for you to fish with live bait in the Territories, but it is a good survival skill to know how to catch loch." This rather ugly, slightly alien looking fish is also known as burbot, eelpout or lingcod. For Native people across the subarctic, the liver of the loch is considered a delicacy. It is an extremely rich source of vitamin D.

George dug around in his pack for a moment and pulled out a night line rigged with a string of size 2 streamer hooks. After tying a beach rock to the far end of the line, he baited each hook with a bit of moose meat and cast the rock into the Mackenzie River. The line extended from above the mouth of Saline Creek along the eddy line between the plume of clear water from the stream and the mottled brown of the Mackenzie River. Though George looked dejected in the morning, when his quest for loch had been foiled by a 10-pound "river" or bull trout that had tangled the night line, I had picked up a few hints about fishing the Mackenzie River. Soon I was taking trout and Arctic grayling from Mackenzie River stream mouths with small spinners and streamers. Fishing the clear water plumes is similar to fishing Pacific estuaries for the elusive sea-run cutthroat trout. Grayling and trout drift in and out of the mouths of the tributaries, hanging along the eddy lines, and sometimes they simply disappear. Unfortunately, the fish that August would simply not rise to the fly.

Late June can be a time of unsettled weather on the Mackenzie River. George and I were stuck in the Native community of Wrigley, waiting out a wind that had been ripping the big river's current to a froth for several days. As it so happens, the caprice of the weather presented me with my first shot at Arctic grayling on a dry fly.

I had flown the length of a small creek near town the year before on a helicopter survey of the proposed route for the Norman Wells oil pipeline. The stream intrigued me, and

so with time on my hands, I took a walk. The brook winds out of the foothills of the Franklin Mountains down the Mackenzie from Wrigley. Spring break-up on the Mackenzie River, annually rearranges the mouth of the creek, as the brook's own spring freshet carves a new channel around the melting mounds of ice pushed into its mouth by the Mackenzie's flood. As I approached, I heard a squeal of delight from the bushes. Crawling over logs and pushing aside the encroaching growth of willows, I found a beaming middle-aged man standing on a bar in the middle of the stream. Seeing me, he inquired, "Did you ever catch a grayling on a dry fly?" "No," I replied, "but I would sure like to try." A moment later, before I could even set up my rod, he had thrust his into my hand and I found myself eyeing up a short riffle. A careful roll cast kept the line away from the grasping willows, as the size 16 Yellow Humpy touched down in a small dimple. Seconds later a flash of purple broke the surface and pulled the fly under. I quickly recovered line and after several short runs and spectacular leaps, I slid the fish up to a bar and slipped the hook from its jaw. A moment after I righted the grayling, it recovered and scurried for cover under an overhanging willow root.

I discovered afterwards that my benefactor was a bored, thirsty electrician working on the airport lighting system. He and his co-workers were waiting for the weekly DC-3 supply plane to bring the parts that they needed to finish the job. By way of repayment, I led him to the co-op store, where we picked up sugar, yeast and raisins so I could teach him the not so delicate art of making three day homebrew. At that time the essential ingredients were all conveniently grouped together on the store shelf for easy one stop shopping. Wrigley was, after all, full of bored, thirsty people. After some brief instructions I left him to make his brew, while George and I hit the river. Later when I ran into him again at the Yellowknife Airport, he told me that just before the batch was done, an RCMP officer in town serving summons to bootleggers had stopped by the electrician's trailer for tea. Despite the telltale odour, the constable had sipped his tea and chatted about nothing in particular, while my benefactor sweated bricks. Undoubtedly, he was enjoying his hosts discomfort as he helped himself to a second cup, but he never mentioned the elicit brew.

When Tom Andrews and I went up the Mackenzie River from Fort Simpson to the Rabbitskin River, I told Tom about the Arctic grayling at the Blackwater. Though it was August, I thought we might be able to repeat the trick. After catching a few northern pike but no grayling, our guide, Leo Norwegian, finally shook his head and said, "Ya, I guess if you want grayling this time of year you need to fish around the heads of islands where the clear water breaks under the willows." On the lower Mackenzie River, the hard fought lessons simply continue as one ferrets out local secrets.

While the river below the confluence of the Liard River is a hard study, the upper Mackenzie is a fisherman's dream.

When biologist Frank Bishop did his pioneering study of Arctic grayling in the mid-1960s, he concluded that Great Slave Lake and the upper Mackenzie River were possibly the best grayling habitat in North America. His only qualification was the potential of the much less accessible Great Bear Lake. Bishop continued that the western end of Great Slave Lake and upper Mackenzie River generally produced the biggest and heaviest fish. If you want consistently large Arctic grayling, the upper Mackenzie River is the place to go.

To protect the fishery of the upper Mackenzie River, catch and release of Arctic grayling has been encouraged by Brabant Lodge, the only facility on the upper river, since the late 1960s. Officially, limits have gone down over the years. In 1974, they were reduced from 10 per day and 10 in possession, to five fish per day and 10 in possession, with a 14 inch limit for Arctic Grayling. The limits for both Arctic grayling and northern pike were dropped again in 1979, when grayling were set at three per day and five in possession, and northern pike dropped from five per day and 10 in possession, to three per day and five in possession. It was at this time that the slot limit of one northern pike over 35 inches was enacted to protect the trophy fishery. Although these regulations have helped maintain the award winning fishery, over the years the average age of a 14-inch Arctic grayling has risen from six to seven years old.

After record warm temperatures in 1989 stressed suckers, Arctic grayling, whitefish and a few northern pike, some fell victim to the Aeromonas hydrophila and Pseudonionus putrifaciens bacteria. It killed droves of fish and left many of the survivors scared. Arctic grayling stocks associated with the Kakisa River run were particularly hard hit. During a one hour trial fishery in the spring of 1989, fisheries officials landed 32 Arctic grayling on the lower

Fishing for Arctic grayling off Brabant Island, Mackenzie River.

Kakisa. A year later the same experiment produced three fish. Although the Lob Stick Island stock which spawns near Brabant Island, were effected to a lesser degree, that fishery is also still recovering. Due to the population crash of the Arctic grayling, the limits were lowered again in consultation with Brabant Lodge, to conserve the breeding stock. During the spawning season there is a zero take/zero possession limit for Arctic grayling in the Kakisa River and the upper Mackenzie River. George Low, the Fisheries Management Biologist for the Department of Fisheries and Oceans who handled the infestation, does not feel that catch and release fly fishing has an impact on the spawn, but stresses the need to carefully handle the fish to reduce the potential for mortality. After the spawn, a one fish per day limit with a total possession of one fish is enforced for Arctic grayling. The limit on Northern pike was dropped to two fish per day with a maximum possession of three. Only one of these can be over 35 inches.

The upper Mackenzie River is the most severely restricted fishery in the NWT, but the result has been the maintenance of a superb trophy fishery.

According to John and Ellen Pollard, the owners of Brabant Lodge, their objective is to minimize the impact of their operation on the river while continuing to provide a quality experience for their guests. In addition to the limits on possession, they have established fixed shore lunch sites and limit the number of guests they service per season. The results of their concern are obvious, the riverbanks are clean and the Arctic grayling are coming back. The trophy northern pike fishery has been maintained for the 30 years the lodge has been in operation. While John does acknowledge that no one has taken a 35-pound northern pike for a number of years, he observed that fish in the high 20s are common and a few each season break the 30 pound mark. He smiled as he noted that recently fly fishermen, angling with single barbless hooks, have been consistently taking larger northern pike than hardware fishermen. The accuracy of his statement was obvious to me on the river. There have been several fly rod tippet class world records taken by lodge guests over the years and from my observation there is every reason to believe more will follow. Canadian Department of

Fisheries and Oceans biologist, George Low believes that because of the success of conservation measures and the strong habitat, the stocks of Arctic grayling will recover and the northern pike are stable.

Beyond their low impact approach to shore lunch and the conservation of the established game fish species, Brabant Lodge is also trying to interest their clients in new species. With the help of Spokane fly shop owner John Propp, they have started to push fly fishing for whitefish as an alternative to grayling. Lake whitefish are as selective as brown trout, fight well and produce delicious smoked meat. My guide Ray Bradshaw, who had a choice of targets, fishes for whitefish on his days off. In the evening, it is not unusual to see one of the guides angling for whitefish near the lodge. That says a lot about the sporting challenge of a species when it draws guys who work with fish day after day.

Part of the puzzle with whitefish are their "short" strikes and their frequent refusal to take high floating dry flies. The answer actually lies in the design of their mouths. Unlike an Arctic grayling which has a mouth located on the front of its face with a jaw hinged like a trout, the mouth of a whitefish is located under the front of their face. As a result, they have difficulty sniping a fly off the surface. When whitefish are rising and yet refuse a dry fly, they are probably taking emergers very near the surface. You can see their strategy if you carefully watch their rises. Their back breaks the surface as they position their mouth to apprehend a nymph on its way to the surface. A no hackle dry, drowned below the meniscus, will often turn the trick.

Memominee, or mountain whitefish, have a feeding cycle very similar to the Arctic grayling but tend to hold in middle water depths and are therefore not normally taken when grayling fishing in the outlet of Great Slave Lake.

Lake trout are found in a few deeper holes in the river. Lake trout and grayling do overlap in the upper section of the river though. The most common species mix on the upper Mackenzie River is Arctic grayling, lake whitefish and northern pike. Walleye are consistently found in a few runs near several small islands. Finding them requires local knowledge.

On my first day at Brabant Island, Ray commented as we pulled from the dock that if a fish was not going to be kept, they prefer that we release it in the water to avoid excessive handling. Knowing that I wanted pictures he offered to help hold the fish near the boat. I smiled and screwed the polarizing filter on my lens. It was a pleasure to cooperate with folks that were serious about resource conservation. Knowing that Brabant Lodge is committed to the conservation of the fishery of the upper Mackenzie River, I am not worried about telling you it is one of the best in the north.

Despite this, it is important to realize that northern fish grow more slowly then their southern brethren. Great Slave Lake grayling sexually mature at six to seven years of age. This compares with three years in Montana and five to six years on the Saskatchewan River in northern Alberta. Late maturity is compensated for by the fact that Arctic grayling live longer in northern waters. A one-and-1/2- to two-pound fish is six to seven years old while a three pounder is an ancient 12 year

Ray Bradshaw with a Mackenzie River Arctic grayling near Brabant Island.

old. Nine years is the average age expectancy for Mackenzie River grayling. The world record fish at 29 and 7/8 inches, 5 pounds, 15 ounces, taken off the East Arm of Great Slave Lake, either had a very big unexpected growth spurt or was an unlikely 13 or 14 years old when it was caught. I hope that fish was very prolific and distributed its genes widely throughout Great Slave Lake.

One afternoon, while fishing off an island near Brabant Lodge, I took a half dozen grayling in the 20 to 22 inch range and a score between 16 and 20 inches. Although we did not weigh the fish, I am sure a couple topped four pounds. Bishop speculates that it is only the older and larger Arctic grayling that hold territory around the upper Mackenzie River islands. Couple this with the fact that they school by age class and you have an explanation of why you find pockets of trophy fish.

Arctic grayling run to their spawning streams as soon as ice jams at the entrances to creek mouths open and allow them passage. This normally occurs in late April on the creeks and rivers that feed the Mackenzie and in June, after the ice has broken up on Great Slave Lake, for the stocks that spawn around the islands in the Mackenzie River itself. The Canadian Department of Fisheries and Oceans has identified at least three separate Arctic grayling stocks in the Mackenzie River between Great Slave Lake and the mouth of the Kakisa River. They spawn at distinct locations and at separate times.

Curiously, grayling and pike are often found spawning together at the same time, in the same water. Apparently the splayed dorsal fin helps them to deter predation by the pike by greatly enhancing their profile.

Fish heading to spawn feed only when food virtually bumps into their nose. The voracious Arctic grayling associated with spawning runs are generally spent fish who have the munchies afterwards. This means that fishing the spawning run is not particularly harmful if you are carefully practicing catch and release. Being practical, half-starved, freshly spawned fish do not taste good.

On the small streams of the Mackenzie Lowlands, the Arctic grayling start feeding on Baetidae nymphs and fish eggs. A Blue-Winged Olive hatch in May is generally the first dry fly fishing of the year in the western NWT. Along the Kakisa River, a large tributary of the Mackenzie River, Giant Stonefly nymphs (Pteronarcyidae), Western Yellow Stonefly nymphs (perlodid) and net-spinning caddisfly nymphs and larva (Hydropsychidae) provide breakfast for the grayling after a long winter under the ice. Gomphidae or club-tailed dragonfly nymphs provide the last ingredient in the big nymph feed along the bottoms of the western NWT spawning rivers. By late June, with rising water temperatures, the spawned out Kakisa grayling drop back into the Mackenzie River as the insects emerge into their adult forms. Caddisflies supplemented by terrestrial ants, beetles and wasps now become the major source of food for the Mackenzie River fish. When the fish are not rising during the summer, they are normally on the bottom feeding on stonefly nymphs. Big Bitch Creek Nymphs, with a piece of split shot clamped on their nose, have saved my day more than once when I could not make a grayling rise to a dry. Spotted and green sedges are the most common caddis variants. Mayflies seem to play a relatively minor role in the graylings' food supply as adults.

Insects form 71% of the food supply for Arctic grayling in the western part of Great Slave Lake and in the upper Mackenzie River. Their diet is rounded out by cisco, slimy sculpin and nine spine stickleback fry and scuds (Amphipoda). Feeding on fish and scuds is less frequent and more opportunistic than their steady fare of aquatic insects.

By way of comparison, on the eastern end of Great Slave Lake along the Stark River near the Chipeywan community of Lutsel'ke, the feeding habits of the Arctic grayling are quite different. Here, the near shore of the lake is dominated by deeper water along the irregular granite outcrops of the Canadian Shield. Colder summer water temperatures result in insects making up only 29% of the Arctic grayling diet. The spring smorgasbord of nymphs found to the west has shrunk primarily to Baetidae and Hydropsychidae. Later, when the fish are rising to emergers and adults, the balance between aquatic and terrestrial insects swings toward floundering land critters. Ciscos, slimy sculpins, nine spine sticklebacks and scuds are more significant in the subsistence base of the eastern fish. Binge feeding on Amphipoda is common. Despite this shift in feeding patterns, caddis are still a very significant element in the grayling diet.

Bishop's study has broad implications a NWT fly box. His study has confirmed many impressions I had formed while fishing in the western NWT. I have found giant stonefly nymphs in streams from the Mackenzie Mountains to the Kazan River. Dragonflies and damselfly nymphs are a common staple. Bishop's discussion on netspinning caddisflies was a revelation to me that caused me to change the way I fished caddis nymphs and pupa. It is obvious that caddis nymphs need to be fished at the bottom and not in mid-water. A less clear but equally important observation is the importance of the proper sizing of flies for Arctic grayling. Arctic grayling do not have particularly large mouths. I have watched good fish have trouble taking nymphs and streamers tied on size 8 and size 10 hooks, even if the fly evoked a strong feeding instinct. Bulky stonefly and dragonfly nymphs are frequently tied on size 2 to size 10 hooks. Generally, the challenge of tying these larger nymphs for Arctic grayling is to adapt your patterns to 2X and 3X, size 12 hooks. The actual bulk of the pattern must be kept to a minimum while using fur and feathers as the grayling uses its dorsal fin to give the illusion of greater size. My solutions include the use of more soft hackle patterns, substituting ostrich and well plucked fur dubbing for chenille, and a single heavy strand of lead or copper lashed along the top of the hook shank for weight instead of wrapping it. Both methods of attaching weight cause the shank to become the fly's keel with the hook safely up and away from the rocks. Tie the fly "up side" down. Variations of the Black Stonefly Nymph and the Assam Dragon allow a smaller fly to project a larger image. Bishop's data indicates that the adult stoneflies and dragonflies are a minor element in the diet of Arctic grayling in the upper Mackenzie River. Despite this, I would still have some Golden Stones and Clubtailed Dragonflies in my fly box, as I have occasionally found them very useful.

This said, the large Arctic grayling of the upper Mackenzie have no problem chowing big size 2 stonefly nymphs. In fact, when I visited Brabant Lodge, I found that nymphing 1/32-ounce jigs tied as Woolly Buggers, and size 2 to size 6 Bitch Creek Stonefly Nymphs netted me a lot of larger Arctic grayling. My friend Dale Freshi has had the same experience a few miles to the southeast on the Kakisa River, during the spring run. On the Mackenzie River this can mean working your fly over the bottom through up to 10 feet of water.

Hook size and bulk can be even more critical for the streamer patterns imitating bait fish. When I tie my various nine spine stickleback patterns for lake trout, I use long shanked size 2 and size 4 hooks, and for smaller grayling they need to be cut back to a size 12. The most effective adaptation I have found for the small stickleback is to use a White and Green Clouser Minnow. Muddlers do a fine job for sculpins at that scale. For ciscos, I use a white tufted muddler head with a silver Mylar body covered with white saddle hackle. When I am feeling creative, I put a single turn of red saddle behind the head for gills. Figure?

Caddis larva quite naturally fall into the size 12 to 14 range, making slight of hand unnecessary. The net-spinning caddis can be imitated with an Olive Brown Caddis larva tied to a bit of white tippet and tethered to split shot. I often avoid the hassle of painting white tippet by simply using a very slow drift along the bottom. A selection of Gary LaFontaine's emergent Sparkle Pupa and Diving Caddis in sizes 12 to 16 are also useful as the season progresses. Take a good selection of patterns for adult caddis. At a minimum, you will want colour and size variations of the Bucktail Caddis, Elk Hair Caddis, Goddard's Caddis,

The dock at Brabant Lodge.

and possibly LaFontaine's Dancing Caddis.

Arctic grayling and walleye tend to be inshore species. Grayling sometimes carry this to the extreme on the Mackenzie River. They are often found hanging out under the willows, over a gravel bottom, or along the shore of an island. Float a beetle under an overhanging willow and see if a grayling snips it. The walleye will frequently respond to a smaller Mega Diver or a Clouser Minnow dredged along the bottom.

Grayling select areas with water temperatures between approximately 45 degrees F (7.5 degrees C) and 53 degrees F (11.5 degrees C). When the fish kills occurred on the Mackenzie River in 1989, water temperature rose above 68 degrees F (20+ degrees C).

Northern pike select similar inshore habitat but seem to prefer slightly warmer water temperatures. Serious pike fishermen drop below the Big Island archipelago to Beaver Lake. On fine summer days, the boats from Brabant Lodge spread out over the weed beds of the lake forming what I jokingly referred to as the pike line. I load my 8 weight with a sinking tip line. Not wanting to overstress the northern pike I hook, I opt to put a steel pike tippet on the front of three feet of 30 pound test. This lets me fight the fish reasonably quickly and release them before they become too tired. The only problem with the steel tippet is having to reset the cable fastener with a pair of pliers every time you want to change flies. I thought I would outsmart the system and put a small brass swivel clip on the end of the tippet to expedite switching flies. On my third cast of the first morning, I saw a flash of

Northern Pike fishing in a Mackenie River backwater along Lobstick Island.

green and silver as my Mega Diver disappeared and line started to scream off the reel. When the fish passed close to the boat, even Ray who sees lots of big fish, got excited and muttered something about it being way over 40 inches and it has got to be 29 or 30 pounds. A minute later, when I tried to turn the fish from the weeds, it was all over. The locking jaw of the clip was bent straight. Cable fasteners do have their place even if the pike don't mind a swivel fastener. Over the next three days, the pike chewed my 18 inches of steel down to about four inches as I brought a range of fish to the boat, many broke 35 inches, a few topped 40 inches and several topped the 20 pound mark. Roger Crawford from Spokane, boated a 28-pound monster up the weed bed from us.

The folks that are looking for tippet class records sandwich their test rated material behind a 30 pound shock tippet that may survive the barracuda-like teeth of a big northern pike.

The treacherous 32-mile crossing of Great Slave Lake from Hay River to the outlet, or the 40-mile trip upstream from the Fort Providence ferry crossing, make the short flight to the Brabant Lodge the best option for fishing the upper Mackenzie River. Watching the Mackenzie River flow by the deck, a dry cabin and bed after a rain squall, Ellen Pollard's great food and the lodge's guides make the Brabant Lodge a great choice. In water as large and as shallow as the upper Mackenzie River, local knowledge can make the difference between a successful trip and going home skunked with a broken motor.

Fishing the Mackenzie River is a unique experience if you love big rivers. The variety and complexity makes for challenges that could last several lifetimes. "Two Faces Of The Mackenzie River" has tried to give you a brief introduction to the variety of potential experience that may await you. I cannot think of another North American grayling fishery that compares to it.

Chapter Thirteen

Deline—Where The Water Flows

Deline is Slavey for "where the water flows" from Great Bear Lake into the Great Bear River. Everything at the end of the arm drifts toward the river.

For the Slavey, or Dene, as they refer to themselves, Deline is one of the most dependable fisheries in the Mackenzie drainage. Simply known as "the fishery" to early traders and explorers, fur trade posts on Great Bear Lake were placed near it. At Deline, white traders without the Dene's hunting skills could survive the winter. In 1825, Hudson's Bay Company factor Peter Warren Dease built a fort at Deline for the British Navy's Second Overland Expedition. The men named the fort after their commander, then Captain John Franklin. There are not many spots in the northwest where 50 men could live off country provisions and winter together without being dispersed into Native hunting camps.

One hundred years later, the significance of the fishery was undiminished when anthropologist Cornelus Osgood wintered near it. His personal account Winter, is a wonderful tale of life at the Great Bear Lake fishery during the 1920s. Osgood was there in an era when winter travel was still done with dog sleds and survival depended largely upon fish hauled through the ice.

Later, in the 1940s and early 1950s, when the Canadian government began to push the Dene of Great Bear Lake to move into a more permanent settlement with a school and medical aid,

they chose to live next to the old site of Fort Franklin. The fishery called Deline would provide for them.

Below the lake, the Great Bear River runs for 80 miles through the stunted black spruce of the Mackenzie Lowlands to Tulita—where its waters join the Mackenzie River by the community of Fort Norman. Along the way, the Great Bear River rolls down the St. Charles rapids. At the water gap, through the Franklin Mountains, it passes the now abandoned Bennet Field Camp of the Northern Transportation Company (NTCL), at the lower end of the old truck portage around the rapids. During the Second World War, uranium yellow cake used by the Manhattan Project for the first nuclear weapons passed this way from the mines near Port Radium on the east end of Great Bear Lake. Today, the end of the portage provides an interesting place to stretch your legs after lunch or to set up a spike camp for a few days of fishing in the rapids.

Visited together, Deline and the Great Bear River provide an outstanding angling destination for fly rod and light tackle fishermen.

While sport fishing lodges have gradually spread to the other arms of Great Bear Lake, Keith Arm and the fishery have remained for the use of the Dene.

With scheduled airline service from both Yellowknife and Norman Wells, the friendly folks at the Great Bear Lake Hotel, and along with local boat rentals, fishing at Deline is a straightforward affair. It is the only place on Great Bear Lake you can easily plan a relaxed paced, do-it-yourself fishing trip with local Native guides. By Great Bear Lake standards, it is even affordable.

Skip trolling for big lake trout around the outlet. You will take enough respectable trout on your fly rod or with light spinning tackle. (The needs of a shore lunch occasionally take precedent over the purity of method.) You are there because Deline offers some of the hottest Arctic grayling fishing in the north. Before the advent of snowmobiles, when the Dene were still running large dog teams, reports indicate that as many as 22,000 Arctic grayling were netted annually from spawning creeks around the fishery. When gas replaced frozen fish as the fuel of choice, the need to take these massive numbers of fish decreased. Despite the heavy historical use of the fishery, the healthy stocks today provide world class angling.

Mature Great Bear Lake Arctic grayling average six to nine years of age, range from 12 to 16 inches in length, and weight from one and a half to two or more pounds. While not uncommon, three-pound fish are certainly not the norm. Prior to 1967, when a fish from the Katseyedie River (a tributary of Great Slave Lake) took the record at 21 inches, five pounds, and seven ounces, an Arctic grayling from Great Bear Lake had held the laurels for a number of years.

Arctic grayling begin rising off the Northwest Company dock, in front of the community, as soon as the ice drifts out in late June or early in July. It is worth the six-mile trip across Great Bear Lake, however, to the outlet of the river, if you want spectacular fishing.

George Pellissey, Andy Hammond and I rolled out of Fort Norman early on the morning of July 1st. Taking a right at Tulita, we headed up the Great Bear River for Deline. The 86-mile trip is normally an excuse to fish the rapids and runs of the Great Bear River and for George to check the salt lick below the St. Charles River for moose, but on that day our pace had to be quick. Isadore Yukon had radioed from Deline to say that great pans of ice were drifting around the end of Keith Arm. The river mouth would stay open as long as the light west wind held, but might drift shut when the breeze dropped. Despite the need to hurry, we stopped at Bennet Field to make tea and to catch a few fish. Over lunch, George described the day he dragged the tug "Lady Franklin" across the portage with a D-8 caterpillar tractor, when NTCL closed down their Great Bear Lake operation in the late 1970s. As we started up the rapids, he told Andy and I about the huge beaver dam that the giant beaver had built across the river when the mythical Dene hero Yamoria chased it from Great Bear Lake. The St. Charles Rapids are the remains of the dam.

Today, hydro-electric developers, not beavers, eye the drop from Great Bear Lake to the water gaps as a potential source of electricity for an energy hungry world.

Near the head of the nine-mile-long St. Charles Rapids, first slush, then small pans of ice began to drift by our boat. It was going to be tight. Our luck held, however, until we reached the old NTCL dock at the far end of truck portage. The horizon line on Great Bear Lake glistened with ice drifting toward us. George slid the boat in below the dock as flows began to grind against the upstream piles.

Navigating on the Great Bear River.

With the boat secure, we surveyed our prospects. Far in the distance, the community of Deline was visible across miles of ice gently riding on the swell. Once convinced we were stuck, our human needs were really elemental—a fire, to cut the chill brought by the returning ice, and Arctic grayling to tempt the pallet. Midsummer's night provided the light.

The river off the abandoned dock had been dredged to provide a channel for the barges and ore boats which used to ply Great Bear Lake. One must cast a fly or light spinner across the old ship channel to the drop-off on the far side, and then let the 6 or 7 knot current swing your line down into the eddy below the dock. This is not the spot for the delicate presentation of a

dry fly. I had a size 12 Mickey Finn on a 4X tippet loaded with split shot. Working our lines around the ice flows was a challenge in which the spinning rods clearly out-classed my sinking tip fly line. If I had only had a full fast sinking line I could have snaked it under the drift ice.

After grayling and tea, we occupied ourselves collecting a pile of firewood for the night. At one point, we threw tar paper on the fire in the vain hope of attracting someone's attention across the lake in Deline. It was not to be, everyone in town was at the Canada Day Celebration by the sports field.

About 9 p.m., the wind shifted slightly and the ice thinned then faded from the river. We quickly crossed to the Deline side before the ice returned and clogged the channel. After laboriously dragging our boat well up from the river, in case the wind piled ice along the shore, we set off on the 10-mile walk around the end of Keith Arm to the community of Deline.

Great Bear Lake is one of the fragments of glacial Lake McConnell which drained from the Lake Athapaskan, Great Slave Lake and Great Bear Lake basins about 6,000 years ago. It was the largest freshwater lake ever known to have graced the North American continent. The lake trout and whitefish which inhabited it formed the parent stock for the countless little fish lakes between Great Bear and Great Slave. Since the catastrophic drop of McConnell, the remaining lakes have gradually assumed their modern levels.

Our walk into the twilight took us along the rim of the ancient beaver pond, as the Dene refer to McConnell beach lines. The terraces are now covered with a thin veil of tundra vegetation. Winter's long grip and winds off the lake have pushed the tree line back almost a half mile from the end of Keith Arm. As we walked along, I noticed that the dwarf willows were only starting to leaf. It is a very short growing season. When I had walked the beach ridges several years earlier, late in August, the willow and bearberries were already brilliant red.

Across the ice, Deline sat glimmering at us, in the long afterglow of evening. The community sits on a high ridge at the edge of the tree line. Exposure makes all the difference around Great Bear Lake. There are spruce two-feet across the butt in the ruins of Fort Franklin next to town. Where I stood looking across, toward

the lights, a 160 year old spruce is only a couple of inches in diameter.

Several of the smaller brooks we crossed had Arctic grayling holding in riffles and pockets. They are slowly making their way back down to the lake after spawning. As we picked our way along the streams looking for crossing places, I marked them in my mind to return and fish.

A half mile short of the community, our path halted at the outlet of Little Gray Goose Lake. It is a wonderful fishery when the trout come in to feed on herring or to spawn, but at 11:30 at night, with the village on the far side, it was less than inspiring. The channel was a mere 45 feet across and only six to eight feet deep but with bits of ice floating in on the swell, swimming seemed out of the question. For the second time that night, we built a signal fire and sat down near the remains of Osgood's cabin to wait for help. My suggestion of an additional three-mile walk around the lake was voted down.

A truck appeared on the far side. It looked like a couple of guys joy riding with their girls. When they saw Andy jumping up and down they waved back. With hand signals they indicated they were going to get a canoe. Later, after a lot of catching up with folks in town, a sleeping bag on Tony Tatti's floor was a welcomed end to a very long day. Isadore had forgotten to tell Tony we were coming today. He had expected us the next day, otherwise he would have left a canoe for us.

Over the next five days, the ice drifted in and out of Keith Arm. When it went out, half of the town ran to set nets. As ice returned, there was a scramble of canoes among the ice pans to pull the nets again.

On the 6th of July, we were finally able to fetch George's boat from across the bay. With the ice gone, the Dene raced to the fishery. Nets work through the ice and in open water, but during the in-between period, life can be hard.

The Fort Franklin archaeological project kept us busy for the next month. Fishing was relegated to the odd evening foray. Finally, near the end of the month, George and I were able to leave Andy with the crew and do some surveying around the river outlet.

A Great Bear River business lunch, amid a day of archaeological testing, demands a quick trip to the middle of the river to fish. Anchored in the heart of the Arctic grayling fishery, four to five casts for four fish were all that was needed for a shore lunch.

Fishing from a stationary boat at mid-channel, anchored in three to five feet of water over a boulder strewn bottom—this is the place where the grayling hold in the swift current. Casting from a boat in the outlet

allows you to cover a broader range of subsurface structures than would be possible from shore or by wading.

Wading is not recommended along the Great Bear River. It is too swift and bone chillingly cold to tempt fate. I recorded water temperatures from 34 degrees F. to 45 degrees F. in July. A trip through the rapids in those conditions is asking for hypothermia or worse. The Great Bear River is big water. Though I am comfortable running a boat in much heavier currents, I always go with a local guide so I can concentrate on fishing. Besides, you cannot beat homegrown knowledge to help along a successful day.

Casting well consistently across the old boat channel requires a good double haul and preferably a shooting taper. My experiences there with a weight forward, sinking tip line convinced me that bigger guns were necessary. Since that time, I have built a very stout, fast action 10-foot, 5 weight rod that is the cat's meow for dry fly

Tony Tatti with a Great Bear River Arctic grayling on the line.

fishing on big water and delivers a fast sinking shooting taper to the grayling on the Great Bear River. Of course the easiest thing to do is to anchor your boat in mid-channel.

Generally, the grayling feed along the bottom. Because of the swift flow, I use a full sinking line with a short leader heavily weighted with shot when casting from an anchored boat. I want the fly to bounce just off the bottom. My casts quarter the river behind the stern. Soft hackle stonefly and caddis nymphs tied in the round are generally good choices. Charles Brooks' Skunk Hair Caddis is an excellent fly for the water.

If we are drifting I will use a sinking tip line with a pair of small streamers that might draw a strike in mid-water, in the interest of being able to pick up and cast more quickly.

Even as I finished writing this description, my memory contradicts my advice, for I remember evenings when the surface has been alive with breaking fish. One night in August, George came over after dinner to tell me about using grasshoppers as Arctic grayling bait. He reveled as he described out-fishing a couple of RCMP constables with live hoppers at the river outlet. They kept yelling over, trying to find out what George was using. He would shrug and hold up another fish, bigger then the last. Before long we were in the boat with a box of Joe's Hoppers and Single-Hank Hoppers. As we plunged the hoppers onto the water, the explosive response convinced me that Arctic grayling love grasshoppers. It was one of those unabashed performances, after which it is hard to convince people that grayling can sometimes be damn selective.

A few years later, I sat in the sunny window of the Great Bear Lake Hotel. It was a January day and I was reading The Compleat Schwiebert while waiting for an airplane that was not coming. I looked up and mused about fishing the Great Bear River. Outside, it was -50 degrees F. A breeze was lofting snow off the ice to create a blizzard about five feet deep. From my perch in the hotel, I could look over the ground effect storm and see the steam rising from the Great Bear River six miles away. The current keeps the upper five miles of the river open through the coldest snaps. It is a characteristic of many good Arctic grayling streams and rivers, that they do not completely freeze in winter. The wanderings of a bored mind led me to wonder if I could catch a grayling at -50 degrees? Not having a fly rod distracted me, and so I wrote fishing writer Ernest Schwiebert a letter in care of his publisher, speculating on the wonders of winter grayling fishing on the Great Bear River. If his secretary was sensible, she would throw the letter away before it bothered her boss. Once again staring across at the river, I had started considering how to de-ice my fly line when the airline agent came in to tell me the plane had turned back to Yellowknife. Knowing the plane would not come until the morning relieved me of sitting in readiness listening for the sound of distant turboprops. I threw my bags back in the room, stopped by the post office to mail the letter, and headed down the hill to scrounge tea and moose meat from Tony Tatti. Moose hunting, now there is a good winter activity. I wondered as I walked toward the Tatti's door if I was going to be stuck in Deline long enough to help Tony haul another one home.

Chapter Fourteen

Dry Flies And Lake Trout—Halcyon Days On Great Bear Lake

Early May on Great Bear Lake is an enchanting time. The long days of spring melt the snow off the lake ice making a freeway for dog teams and snowmobiles. Half the people in Deline were out travelling on the land. Tony Tatti and I were getting ready to take advantage of the weather by setting fuel caches for use by our boats later in the summer. We planned to be on the water, headed for Grizzly Bear Mountain, shortly after the five-feet-thick ice melted from Keith Arm early in July. The trick is to be on the lake soon after the shore ice goes out, but before the centre of the lake clears. Old ice floating around in the middle of the lake diminishes the fetch of open water available for the wind to kickup really big waves. The theory works and besides, right after the ice goes is the best time to chase lake trout with a fly rod.

As we hauled drums from the community fuel dump to the beach, Tony and I mused about the Arctic grayling moving under the lake ice toward their spawning streams. Grayling will hang off the creeks until they can leap over the last ice dam into their home water sometime in early June. Below the lake, along the perpetually open Great Bear River, the grayling will start for their spawning beds by the middle of May. Around the first of June, they will be off the redd and hungry as spring bears. Unfortunately, long before that happens, I will be back in Yellowknife, absorbed with the details of the approaching summer.

As Tony and I fingered the map, calculating fuel consumption for a pair of 18-foot aluminum skiffs, I asked about fish creeks. It seemed a logical question as creeks provide a sheltered break to land a small boat when the surf is too high on the gravel beaches. Half listening from across the room, Tony's father Francis piped in about the best places to put our fuel. Tony and his dad lapsed into Slavey as their fingers slid back and forth over the topographic maps. Francis was right of course, the bays he suggested were much safer for our drums than creek mouths. We wanted to be able to get to our fuel in any weather. It was imperative the 10-gallon kegs were placed above the high storm line. Nevertheless, they had to be close enough to the beach so that we would not have to carry them too far. When you drop off barrels with a snowmobile, it is easy to forget how far you have to lug them later. Previously, I limped around Great Bear Lake with a twisted back from unloading a 45-gallon drum out of a skiff. This year, I vowed to find a better system. Francis had suggested stashing the 10-gallon kegs along our route. It would mean lighter loads in the boats and fewer bruised fingers and backs.

Finished with the fuel caches, Francis turned to me and smiled as he pointed to several creeks on the map. In broken English he said "Good trout. Old guys you're travelling with will stop for tea." I smiled back and kidded Francis that he must be a young 85 to call a couple of fellows in their 70s old.

Francis was correct. Peter Baton and George Kotakin would stop at all the fish creeks around the southwest corner of Great Bear Lake to tell their story of Dene life on the land. Grizzly Bear Mountain is sacred to the Dene as the spiritual home of the big brown bears known as Sah cho in Slavey.

Later, as I helped Tony lash drums on his sled for the fuel shuttle, I thought about lake trout on a fly rod. I take them regularly with nymphs and streamers, but dry flies are unpredictable. I concluded that being in the right place at the right time was a factor I often negated by simply fishing when I had time. What a pleasant task—a job that, in part, required me to learn about the traditional Native fisheries of Great Bear Lake.

Back in Yellowknife, I ran through my notes on lake trout from previous years. Caddis imitations are the key. Generally, when I had taken lake trout on a dry fly before, it had been a caddis fly pattern that had turned the trick. My previous successes, however, had normally been in moving water. How was I going to crack that huge lake and break the streak of bad luck that had followed me around Great Bear Lake the previous August?

Dry flies and lake trout. On the Kazan River, I had used size 12 to size 16 Nelson's Caddis flies for three- to six-pound trout. Tied with caribou hair, it was a very buoyant pattern that did well in the eddies and deep pockets of the Kazan. It obviously deserved a spot in my Great Bear fly box. What I needed was a very adaptable pattern that could be field trimmed to meet the moment. Previously, I had watched lake trout both gently snip big caddis from the meniscus and thrash after a travelling sedge, skittering along the

surface in preparation for takeoff. Being a lazy tier, I wanted to imitate both states with one pattern. In a flash of insight, I tied several Goddard's Caddis patterns from size 10 to size 14 in olive and mottled-gray and brown, but I did not trim them. If I wanted a fluttering caddis, I nipped a few hairs to create flapping wings. For a sedentary insect, I trimmed the body into the tight triangular tent characteristic of a resting sedge. The Goddard's Caddis is a very stable fly that floats well and can be skated without rolling over. I felt so pleased with myself. I stuffed a score into a box for the trip. To make sure my caddis selection was complete I included a mix of Caribou and Elk Hair Caddis in sizes 10 to 14, and Deer Hair Caddis from size 16 to size 18.

I finished out my dry fly selection with Midges, Adam's (including a parachute variation), Blue-Winged Olives, Royal Wulffs, Black Gnats, Mosquitoes, Red and Yellow Humpys, Bivisibles, and light Hendricksons. Keeping with a northern theme, I used musk ox kiviut (wool) for dubbing on my Adam's. Raw kiviut is a lovely, fine wool rich in lanolin, which comes in a range of colours from very dark brown to cream. It makes for very buoyant flies, and dyes nicely to a range of earthy colours. Black Ants, Beetles, Grasshoppers, Hair Mice, and a blue bottle imitation formed my terrestrial selection.

I always carry a good selection of soft hackle Partridge and Orange, and brown, yellow, green and peacock herls in sizes 12 to 18. Soft hackles with white pantyhose shucks trailing behind the fly are useful. I had recently added LaFontaine's antron skirted Emerging Caddis Pupa to my mid-water selection. Now LaFontaine's Emerger and

Diving Caddis are permanent additions to my assortment.

A range of Pheasant Tails, Hare's Ear Nymphs and Caddis Pupa are a necessity for Arctic grayling. Since I fished the Prince River near Baker Lake, I now also include a few size 12 Red Stonefly Nymphs when fishing on NWT waters. I round out the nymphs with a big black stonefly and dragonflies tied upside down. This lets the hook shank become the keel as the bend bumps along the bottom.

Despite my intent, on this trip, to focus on dry flies, I did not neglect streamers. I was quite proud of my variations of the nine spine stickleback and was anxious to try them on Great Bear. Although it has not been widely imitated by streamer patterns, the nine spine is a major forage fish in the northern food chain of lake trout. Out of fly shop bins, the best imitation I have found was an Olive Matuka streamer with a natural grizzly wing. The pattern works, but was not quite the right colour. The dorsal side of a nine spine stickleback is pale to olive green with dark barring. Beneath the nine spine, it is typically silver. Breeding males often have black bellies and white pelvic fins. During spawning, both genders may develop a reddish tinge around the head. As spawning occurs during the summer, the mating variations are obviously relevant to the lake trout fishermen.

As I set out to create my own patterns for the lowly nine spine stickleback, I knew I would need variations that would work for both lake trout and Arctic grayling. This required a range that spanned hook sizes 2 through 12. My first attempt had been a sculpin-like fly with a green and white spun hair head and a silver Mylar body backed with a pale green matuka wing. Tied on a long shank size 2 streamer hook, it emulates the two- to two-1/2-inch length of a mature stickleback. This heavily weighted fly is best suited for use with a sinking line on offshore structures. A nice start, but I wanted a fly that would cast more gracefully. This led to stickleback "light". It is essentially a standard Matuka Streamer with a silver Mylar body, a green grizzly saddle hackle wing and a green soft hackle head. The pattern works nicely on size 2 to size 10 heavy shank streamer hooks. Hackle and wing colours combine a range from pale to dark green. It is tied sparsely so that the weight of the hook will take the fly down. When I tried the prototype stickleback "light" out on Bighill Lake, near Yellowknife, it seemed to draw trout from out of nowhere. The spawning male was imitated by replacing the silver Mylar body on the "light" with a darker shade of Mylar and a single turn of red hackle behind the head. On my return from caching gas along Great Bear Lake, I set to work on a final variation, a size 12 Clouser nine spine stickleback for Arctic grayling. (see Plate)

The slimy sculpin is a favourite forage fish of lake trout. It is imitated by stocky, mottled dark brown, sculpin patterns. Whatever pattern you choose for your sculpin, it should have a relatively flat spun hair head. A Brown Muddler Minnow works well on smaller hook sizes. Adult slimy sculpin reach a maximum size of about three inches. A long shank, size 2 streamer hook is the largest required.

Bear Lake herring are the major food source for lake trout on Great Bear Lake. Ranging from 8 to 12 inches, imitations of the adult herring slip into the range of trolling flies. I occasionally think about getting some of the extremely long shank hooks used in New England style streamers for a Great Bear herring pattern. Currently, however, I use a Silver and White Zonker, or a white chenille body, flanked with white saddle hackle, and a turn of red saddle under a white saddle head, as my stock herring patterns. I carry a range of sizes, from size 2 to size 12, of herring streamers. (The smaller sizes are for Arctic grayling which are known to feed on the fry.)

Beyond the imitations of recognized lake trout bait fish, I always add Mickey Finns, Multi Marabou Muddlers, Deceivers and Marabou Streamers. Attractor patterns are often as effective as the best executed imitation.

Our trip in 1991 took us off water well-known to anglers familiar with Trophy Lodge on Smith Arm, Plummer's Lodge on Dease Arm, or the Arctic Circle and Branson's Lodges on McTavish Arm of Great Bear Lake. Parts of Keith and McVicar arms are fished by sport anglers out of Neiland Bay/Great Bear Lodge on the south shore of Great Bear Lake or on trips from Deline, but they are not as famous as the other parts of the lake.

The southwest corner of Great Bear Lake is dominated by Grizzly Bear Mountain. Rising between Keith and McVicar arms, Grizzly Bear Mountain is a long low limestone hill which rises about 700 feet above Great Bear Lake. Unlike the spectacular undulating granite bedrock of the Canadian Shield which plunges down to the shore along the east end of Great Bear Lake, Grizzly Bear Mountain rises gently out of the ancient beach lines of glacial Lake McConnell. Along

the shore, the moss covered sand terraces wind through open pine forests. They provide wonderful places to stretch your legs after lunch. Coasting along the shore in a small boat, I am always struck by the rising perspective of the windblown beaches giving way to the spruce forests under the shadow of the mountain. Over the years, its piscatorial and scenic delights have made it a place I look forward to returning to.

Most of the drift ice in Keith Arm had blown out around the first of July, a mere week earlier. Pans stuck to shore near town were still dropping prismatic candles of ice that chimed as they washed together in the gentle swell. Further out, the white edge of the main flow was floating on the eastern horizon. Light waves, warped by the interplay of solar heat and cool water, caused the distant ice to loom above the lake in high mirage. It looked like one could sail across the lake beneath the ice. Practically speaking, however, the ice front was 20 miles east and well away from our planned route. Its continued presence suggested that the threatening northeaster would not build big waves. Mirages along the south shore, six miles away, made the arm look like a narrow channel. The sights and sounds of winter's final retreat were still around us as Tony Tatti and I muscled the skiffs down their log skids into Great Bear Lake.

After a miss-start, when a last minute gear check necessitated a final trip to the co-op store for more spark plugs, John Tetso turned the lead boat from shore and headed across Great Bear Lake. Though a one p.m. start seemed late to me, at the height of summer with its near perpetual daylight, early afternoon was only the start of a day that would end 12 hours later as rosy twilight back-lit rising lake trout.

Surfing the second boat on John's wake, Tony and I settled back and let him carry us across the lake. Laying low, I ducked out of the chilling airstream that flowed over the boat and let the sun heat my flotation jacket and wind pants. I must have dozed as I jerked my head up when Tony performed a banked turn to bring us onto a new course along the south shore. Behind us, I watched the head of the Great Bear River fade into the distance. Now, with the flow of forest, beaches and rivulets to watch, I settled down for the ride to Rock Creek where we would stop for tea and limber our rods.

When the lake water is still especially cold right after the ice goes out, there is more food in the relatively warm water coming into the lake from the tributaries. Lake trout come into the creek mouths to feed on the early caddis and stonefly hatches. Throughout the season lake trout in Great Bear Lake tend to be found in shallow areas near shore. As a consequence they have a much higher intake of terrestrial insects in addition to ciscos and sculpins The lakers hanging off the mouth of the creek promised to be the first trout lunch of the trip.

As the boats nosed into the gravel flanks of the stream mouth, they scattered large brown sedges drifting in the back eddies. A little further out, I caught the shadows of trout along the drop-off. While John started a fire and broke out the grill, Tony and I strung rods. His spinner quickly provided lunch, while I awaited my chance for a nice fish that was slowly working its

way into the creek mouth. It was lazily snipping the big caddis from the surface. I stopped fidgeting by nipping the modeled brown Goddard's Caddis into the correct half-flight shape of an insect trying its new wings.

My fly disappeared into a dimple as I heard the filets from Tony's trout start to sizzle in the pan behind me. A few minutes later, I slipped the hook and watched a beautiful eight-pound lake trout fin its way slowly back to the depths as John called, "Come and get it". Libby's beans, fresh bannock, and trout topped off with lots of hot tea—now that's a shore lunch.

Later, we circled Manitou Island which resembles the stone head of a swimming wolf. According to Dene legend, a woman shaman, long ago, drove the wolf from a cave on the main land. As the beast fled across the lake she turned it to stone.

The shadows of trout flashed against the shallow reefs around the island as we circled seeking the right angle for a picture. Unfortunately, dark clouds to the west suggested we should move on. Heavy rain caught up with us shortly as we passed wolf tail shoal. For the next three hours we slogged on through line squalls and driving rain that ripped the waves to a froth. Chilled to the bone, we eventually decided to camp at the north end of the nine-mile-long Johnny Hoe portage. The track runs along old beach lines on the back side of Grizzly Bear Mountain from Keith to McVicar Arm. Before the advent of outboard motors, it saved paddlers from an 85-mile paddle around the mountain to the Johnny Hoe River fishery at the base of McVicar Arm. As I crawled from the boat I noticed ragged cracks of blue in the blackened sky. The break restored my humor enough to let me

Fly camp on the shore of Great Bear Lake.

kid Tony about his hand having been frozen to the tiller. By the time we were ready to pitch the white canvas wall tents and set up the wood stoves, the rain pattered to a halt. Slowly the heat of the stoves and our steaming clothes turned the tents into saunas. Hot tea finished our restoration.

Leaning on their bed rolls, George and Peter began to tell stories about pulling a 25-foot clinker built, cedar plank canoe across the portage on log rollers. They laughed at my skeptical glance and promised to show me the canoe when we reached the far side. Later, Peter and I walked down the trail looking at the remains of old portage carts and boat rollers until he decided he had gone far enough for an old man. The hand carved wheels and skids must have been positively diabolical to have pushed and pulled across the portage. As we broke out of the trees coming back down onto the beach, I caught a glimpse of a rise far out in the bay. The concentric curves ebbing out from the strike sparkled in the last glow of evening.

A brisk breeze grew with dawn's early light. During breakfast, the chop picked up and the wind blew the tops off the whitecaps. More

wood for the stove and a fresh pot of coffee signaled we had decided to wait out the blow. Behind the rattling tent, the willows doubled and the black spruce creaked under the strain of the variable gusts. Later, Tony and I wandered inland to explore the old beach ridges and fetch firewood while the Elders drank tea and talked about the giant grizzly sow that once inhabited the mountain. It was early afternoon before the swell lengthened and we could warp our boats off the beach.

With the wind down, the swell continued to settle as we skirted the coast on our way to Preble Bay. John ducked into a fish creek along the way to procure dinner. I took a nice five- or six-pound fish on a size 8 "stickleback light". The fish bore up from along a drop-off in the dissipating current off the brook. George and Peter smiled at my fly rod. What will the whiteman try next!

We stopped for the night on a small island tucked into the mouth of Jupiter Bay. The island is a crescent of raised gravel bars covered with stunted spruce and caribou lichens. Tucked into the central lagoon, our boats were safe from the worst blows.

After heaps of lake trout fried in chicken Shake and Bake, I gave everyone a good chuckle when I tried to sneak around a colony of gulls to cast into a school of bait fish they were feeding over. The birds were unimpressed by the logic that I was only interested in the lake trout rolling in the herring. As they swooped and screamed, I ducked back into the trees trying to stay below their dives. At least they were not Arctic terns. Across the cove, the guys were clutching themselves.

The previous year Tony, Gordon Hamre (from Yellowknife), and I had spent a bitterly cold few days in late August pinned down on the beach behind the island. Gordon and I both came home with pneumonia. Subsequently locked in the house by a determined wife and a visiting mother, I had to ditch plans for an Arctic charr trip to the Tree River on the coast. This time we had a balmy summer evening when our mosquito nets provided all the cover that was required. Peeking out of my sleeping bag from the crest of the island, the lake was gossamer, trimmed in orange. That night, Great Bear was the most peaceful place on earth.

East of Jupiter Bay, the forests along shore open up. There is less black spruce and more jack pine. The high ground drops inland letting the old beach ridges wind gently through stands of pine. We stopped for lunch by a creek on the eastern tip of Grizzly Bear Mountain. It flows down from a perpetual ice field tucked against the low hills. Later we passed an old saw mill, left from the construction of the mines at Port Radium on the east end of the lake in the 1930s. They must have hauled the lumber off with cat trains in the winter as it would be tough to get a barge into the mill. The gentle terrain inland translates to long shallow beaches that are difficult to get off if the wind comes up. We stopped for the night at a creek mouth that affords the only deep water approach along this section of shore. The wave washed gravel bars along shore cover preserve ice all summer. After trout and sliced potatoes baked in foil, I slipped on my hip boots and waded to the drop-off. I quickly missed two strikes on a herring streamer, then lost the fly on a rock. Next I bumbled a hit on the "stickleback light" before landing a nicely coloured four- to five-pound fish. The lakers are not as big as the fish we took on the other side of Grizzly Bear Mountain, but I am never one to complain about a four-pound trout. With the weather on a roll, we had another beautiful night. Once again we hung out under our bug nets.

Moving down McVicar Arm, we stopped for lunch at old Andre's cabin before George took me to see the big cedar canoe near "Old Ye'dza's" place, close to the portage. He was right. That canoe must have been a beast to drag over the trail lashed on a dog toboggan bumping along on log rollers.

We spent the night at William Mackenzie's shack near a fish creek. Tiring of trout, George and Peter set a net for whitefish tonight. Late in the evening, as the sun took its brief dip below the horizon, I took a couple of small whitefish on a size 14 Yellow Humpy. The guys opted to wait for the big fish from the net, so I slipped the hook both times. Dry fly fishing for whitefish always seems like a late night activity. As far as many Sahtu Dene are concerned, the southwest end of McVicar Arm, near the Johnny Hoe River is one of the best fisheries on the lake. In the old days it was home to many of the people who now live in Deline. Despite their change of address, they still spend a lot of time hunting and fishing in the area. The cabins pass from one generation to the next.

After poking around McVicar Arm all day, we camped in a willow hell hole known as Archie Why Island. It is named after a white trapper who froze to death nearby and was subsequently eaten by his dogs. The dogs would have been quicker than the bugs that tried to carry us off bit by bit that night. To be fair, the sandy shallows around the island were so warm that I indulged myself and took a real bath. By Great Bear Lake standards, swimming in warm water is not a common occurrence.

The next day, we headed east along the south shore of McVicar Arm, back into the cold lair of the lake trout and grayling.

That evening, I got into my first Arctic grayling of the trip. We had camped early at the Hunter and Trapper Association's cabin to escape the heat of day. Despite rumours that summer on Great Bear Lake is marked by two weeks of poor ice skating, it does on occasion get so hot that only mad dogs and Englishmen go out in the noonday sun. As I sat under one of the few spruce trees left near the cabin, half reading, my stupor was broken by first one, then several rises. Despite our view of the weather, it was not too hot for the fish. Donning hip boots and grabbing my 6 weight rod, I waded out to my strap buckles. Another inch and the lake would have cooled my legs. Normal 50- to 60-foot casts simply would not reach the sporadic rises along a distant drop-off. Calling on my meager abilities to double haul, I got another 20 feet and started to consis-

tently hit the drop-off. The fish were cruising and so it was a matter of letting the fly drift until I spotted dimples nearby and then, I twitched the size14 Olive Goddard's Caddis a couple of times and waited for the next rise and repeated the process. Over the next five or six hours, amid leg warming and coffee breaks, I caught and released a baker's dozen of two-pound Arctic grayling.

Picking the right boots has plagued me for years. My normal footwear in the north is calf-high rubber boots that are big enough to stuff with extra socks and felt insoles. Over the years, I have debated taking a pair of chest-high waders along but I always shy away from wearing them in a boat. If you go in the water, they are nothing but trouble. In the end I normally carry a pair of heavy rubber hip boots that are a size too large and have the calf straps ripped out so that they come off very easily. They are great for working boats on and off the beach, and will generally get me out far enough to cast to the drop-offs. Knowing I will probably trash them crawling through the bush, I generally opt for the cheap Chinese ditch boots and lots of rubber patching material. I normally wear Carhart bib overalls because they will take lots of abuse and dry very quickly. When I am going wading, I put a pair of polar fleece pants on underneath. The combination generally keeps me from becoming hypothermic. If the weather goes to hell, I can layer the above under industrial strength Helly Hanson chemical retardant rain gear and an orange flotation jacket with an exposure diaper. The hip boots go under the rain pants so that they don't fill up with water. When the going gets really tough the cuff gets wrapped with duct tape for that chest high effect. Talk about a walking Gumby. Somehow the advantages of casting a two-ounce rod are lost in the process. I should simply fish an old 10-foot Leonard Light Salmon, it would fit in better.

Despite waxing about the joys of bad weather, the hot temperatures and bluebird sky continued. Moving northeast onto the rockier limestone shores around Gordon Point, the shallow foreshore gave way to the sharp bedrock drops more typical of the Canadian Shield further east. At lunch, I sat on a pinnacle and watched large Arctic grayling nosing around the rubble beneath. The fish were nymphing in mid-water on an insect too small to pickup from my vantage. Carelessly, I sank a size 22 Peacock Herl Nymph onto the rocks below the fish. As I slowly raised it, a lovely 16-inch fish nipped it. The grayling leapt with abandon, sending shimmers of blue sunlight off its scales. A few moments later, I slipped the hook and watched it nose down for the cover of the limestone boulders below.

Moving north, we spent the afternoon coasting along the Leith Peninsula toward Great Bear Lodge. Due to the confusion of a change of ownership, the lodge did not open in 1991. Thus following accepted local custom, we sacked out in the guide shack for the night.

Great Bear Lake had been sitting under a large stationary high pressure area for the last few days. As I watched the appearance of high clouds slide cyclically across the northern horizon, I suspected we were in for a drastic weather change. Against the backdrop of the building front, a high black V of geese marked an early flock already headed south from the Barren Lands. The 25th of July felt early for the first

signs of autumn. Shortly after dawn we heard the telltale whine of the wind in the eves. Before the breakfast coffee was ready, a westerly was blowing the tops off the whitecaps. By early afternoon, the weather vane had come around to the northeast.

There was more change in my life that day than weather. A radio message from Yellowknife relayed the news that my wife's transfer had come through. She would be leaving for Cripple Creek, Colorado shortly. On a high ridge behind the lodge, I reflected on what might be my last trip to Great Bear Lake, for awhile, as I considered the implications of living only a short distance from the headwaters of the South Platte River in the Rockies.

As the low settled in over Great Bear, the rain began to fall. When Tony radioed his father in Deline that night, Francis told him the wind was dropping on the west end of the lake. Awhile later he called back to say that the ceiling had dropped to the ground. The low had stalled. I could almost see the fish starting to rise out in the protected nooks and crannies of the bay south of the lodge. Despite my dedication to dry flies, most of my lake trout have been taken with streamers and nymphs.

Out of the growing gloom, an unmistakable note in the air foretold the approach of an old Single Otter float plane. Droning toward us from the northeast, the pilot was playing with the margins to reach the lodge. A few minute later, Tony and I cleated the lines as Chummy Plummer and a couple of his new partners jumped down to inspect the lodge. In a deal including Native groups, the Government of the NWT, and Plummer's Lodges, all of the lodges on the lake came under a common management in 1992. The economics of scale will help offset the enormous costs of operating on Great Bear Lake. As Chummy walked by the guide shack, he quipped, "I should have brought you boys a couple of buckets of tar for the roof. It doesn't look like you're going anywhere for awhile." With the ceiling falling, he lifted off for his main lodge on Dease Arm. Peter glanced up at the departing plane and shrugged as he continued to tumble lake trout filets in a bag of Shake and Bake. A moment later he muttered something about tarring the roof.

Late in the evening, the overcast sky broke briefly, drenching the world in polarized light, filtered through an electrically charged sky. The bayfront of the lodge disappeared opening the lake's secrets. It was as if looking into the lake through a huge pair of Polaroid sunglasses. Watching trout glide by, I wanted to grab my rod but the threatening sky to the west suggested it might not be wise to wave a graphite rod over my head. Even as Tony and I marveled at the still eerie light, the black clouds surrounded us. A flash of lightening signalled the onslaught. The downpour finally subsided around noon the next day. Briefly, the wind dropped and the lake started to calm down. Before we could contemplate packing camp, however, the torrent struck again. Finally at 5 in the evening, after three days (when all we had to do was fish), camp was broken and we headed for Preble Bay in the shadow of Grizzly Bear Mountain. The sky was again threatening as we tucked into the lagoon to regain the campsite we had used seven days earlier. Preble Bay is a lovely place. Open spruce forests run down the beach ridges to the shore, framing the bay and its islands. In a storm, the big

island is a safe vantage from which to watch the Great Bear rage.

The sea subsided overnight, leaving us shrouded in dense fog. Shivering in the chill of an early fall morning, I fumbled to get the coffee started. It was simply too thick to travel. Over the trappers' radio we learned that the entire Mackenzie was socked in. Generally, being beached was no hardship as we fished constantly. Today, however, our luck failed and there were no fresh fish. With our big wall tents firmly pitched, we laid around the wood stove, downing countless pots of tea, and telling stories as mist drifted by the door.

The next morning the dense gloom made sunrise simply a change in the shade of gray. Tired of sitting, everyone was glancing over their shoulders looking for a break. Finally, a light breeze broke the fog up late in the morning. Packing quickly, we started on the long trip back to Deline. Hours later, a rising sea caused us to stop for lunch at a fish creek. I took my final lake trout of the trip on another Goddard's Caddis. Despite all my efforts over the previous 11 days, I did not consistently take lake trout with dry flies. Thank God for streamers. During the three or four hours it took the weather system to pass, we alternated between fishing and feeding the fire.

This creek has two quite distinct populations of lake trout that drift in and out of its mouth. One is characterized by dark backs and a red/orange underside. Their flesh is bright red. The other has lighter green backs and more silver stomachs. By contrast, they have white meat. As we compared the filets, Peter and George began to talk about the various local strains of lake trout around Great Bear Lake.

Listening to them, I recalled the variety of fish taken during our trip, and asked if they thought that many of the creeks had distinct lake trout populations. They nodded, that is what they had been trying to tell me. Having read about the distinct lake trout strains that still inhabit parts of Lake Superior, it all made sense. After the trip, when I read more on the of natural history of the Northwest, I discovered that George and Peter were not simply a couple of very observant guys. They were expressing the broad base of aboriginal environmental knowledge that has been transmitted generation to generation through Native oral traditions.

Northern Ojibwa who were collecting natural history specimens for the Smithsonian Institution in the 1850s, suggested a species split in lake trout of Lake Superior based on the seasonality of spawning. Although seriously debated by scientists at the time, lake trout are now all considered a single species. The historic observations of the Ojibwa reflect a subtle knowledge of the variability between the strains of Lake Superior fish. Peter and George's descriptions of lake trout strains on Great Bear Lake, like the Ojibwa example, reflects a knowledge of the Keith Arm fishery born from generations of experience by the Sahtu Dene. Half the fun of travelling in the north for me, is hanging out with hunters who have spent their whole life living off the land. When Peter and George are around, being stranded on a beach is not a hardship as every place has a story.

Late in the evening the system passed and we pushed on for a hot shower and a warm bed in Deline. By the time we drank tea and told Tony's father Francis about the trip, another day had passed.

During a recent visit back to Deline, John Tetso and I sat in his truck and looked out across the windblown ice of Great Bear Lake. As the wind swirled around the tires we recalled that last trip together. Summer had been upon us then, even as the last vestiges of winter ice drifted on the eastern horizon. The weather had been too warm for jackets as we loaded the boats down by the old Hudson's Bay Company dock.

Those sultry days seemed far away in the gray gloom of mid-winter twilight. A dense cloud cover was keeping the temperature mild, but it had also eliminated all shadows and left the world in flat gray tones without vertical contrast. Black trees on the far shore blended with the steely gray sky and white snow on the lake to form a homogeneous oneness. Out on the lake it was hard to tell if a snowdrift was a bump or three feet tall. Although blowing snow is the common image of a whiteout, more frequently it results from a lack of shadow and vertical contrast. Pilots lose their depth perception and fly into lakes while people on the ground trip over snowdrifts. The black ice of the graded winter road across Great Bear Lake, stretched to infinity as the spruce trees stuck into the snowdrifts to mark its edges became dark pin pricks along the track behind us.

As John turned his truck off the ice road and drove up the beach into town, we finished our reminiscences that were but a prelude for planning our next trip. Below Great Bear Hotel, I spotted Tony's overturned skiffs, poking through the snow, where not so long ago John had swung the lead boat from shore and led the way across the lake.

Chapter Fifteen

Johnny Hoe River

I am largely a catch and release trout fisherman. Oh, I keep a couple now and then for a shore lunch, but generally I slip the hook and watch them swim away. Most self-proclaimed catch and release fisherman, however, also have a delicious black side. Those who acknowledge it love to eat fresh fish. The signs range from hoarding secrets recipes for Beer Battered Bluegills, Blackened Bass and Trout Almandine, to carrying a wicker creel tinged with the smell of mint. On trips to Alaska they bring back lots of smoked salmon. Of course, most people assume the greatest delight is trout sizzling in a pan. Maybe. Among the folks I travel with, walleyed pike is the preferred meal. Trout are fun to catch, but they don't compare to delicate walleye filets dusted in corn meal and lightly fried in bacon grease over an open fire.

My fascination with pickerel started years ago on the Hayes River in northern Manitoba. Before I went north to work, I had heard rumours about spectacular speckle trout fishing. When I arrived in the Cree community of Oxford House, I was at first disappointed to learn from Thomas Chubb Jr., a man who would become my guide and travelling companion, that the big brookies were in the Gods River, 70 miles south. My neighbour Ralph Weenusk told me to put my fly rod away and come walleye fishing. We had spectacular sport on light spinning gear and hand-lining red and white spoons using a milk can as an open face spinning reel. Milk can spinning for big northern pike was particularly inspirational. Later, the condensed milk became a key ingredient for pike chowder. After a good evening, we retired to the beach and sat around a fire frying walleye for half the night. With a full stomach, Thomas would tell me tales of guiding on Gods River for speckles. He habitually ended by suggesting we should portage over to Gods from Knee Lake sometime. Of course we never faced the overland trek. It required humping a canoe for miles in and out of sloughs and small lakes.

After I left Manitoba, I went back to being a trout fisher. A few years ago, however, I was hanging out in the small Dene community of Trout Lake, NWT, with Joe Punch. In exchange for helping to haul 100-feet of net from under five-feet of lake ice, Joe offered me a couple of lake trout for my trouble. Catching my glance at the fish box, he laughed and offered me walleye instead. Though it had been a number of years since I had had walleye, the thought made my mouth water. As we stood throwing the frozen fish from his toboggan into the deep freeze, Joe mused that a feed of lake trout was good once in awhile but you could raise a family on whitefish and walleye.

Unfortunately, because they run deep most of the year, walleye are generally the sport of tackle fishermen. When I want to combine fly fishing with the best of shore lunch, I have to pick my spot very carefully.

The Johnny Hoe River is an open secret that people in Deline had been telling me about for years. It seems that everyone in the western Arctic knows about it but few people actually get there. Tucked into the southwest corner of Great Bear Lake at the base of McVicar Arm, it is located safely outside the range of the operating lodges on Great Bear. Forget it. Your guide can not run you down to catch walleye for lunch.

With the settlement of the Sahtu Dene and Métis Comprehensive Land Claim Agreement, much of the land along the Johnny Hoe River is now private. Though there are public access provisions in the claim, the best way to fish there is to make arrangements in Deline for a local guide. In the good old days, parties used to treat a trip to the Johnny Hoe River as a voyage to the end of the world. The odd assumption, "We're from Wisconsin and therefore do not need fishing licenses," landed one group in Dutch with Walter Bayha, the Renewable Resources Officer in Deline. Walter is a nice guy but don't mess around on his lake.

Other folks have underestimated their gas requirements and have had to hire a boat by radio from Deline to haul out a load of fuel. Rescue in the great Northwest is not cheap. Hiring a local outfitter like Morris Modeste is a sound investment in your northern adventure. When planning the trip, however, allow a little time as you pass through Deline to decompress. Life in the north moves at its own pace.

From my perspective, travelling with my old friend Tony Tatti and the Deline Dene elders made my trip to the Johnny Hoe River. Their stories of life on the land will change your perspective of trackless unexplored wilderness. "Wilderness", once chimed George Pellissey, a companion from Fort Norman, "only exists if you don't know how long we have lived here."

Your Dene guide will either take you out by boat to the mouth of the river or you can make arrangements to fly into Lac Ste. Therese, 20 miles from the mouth. Travelling fast and light, it is a two-day boat trip from Deline to the Johnny Hoe River. If you fly, you need to strap a canoe to the floats of the plane or pack a suitable raft. Normally, people float to the mouth and radio for a pick up. The truly adventurous fishermen, however, might paddle back to town after crossing the nine-mile portage across the base of Grizzly Bear Mountain. Once on Keith Arm, you can fish your way to the outlet of the Great Bear River and then coast on into Deline. Along the 94-mile trip, you will get a great shot at lake trout and Arctic grayling near creek mouths and along offshore drop-offs. The downside is the portage and the amount of time spent on the beach waiting for the lake to calm down. You will be crossing land owned by the Deline Lands Corporation. It will take permission to make the trip. Of course if you go out by boat, you will get to fish Great Bear Lake along the way.

Morris Modeste runs the only organized guiding service in Deline. The Great Bear Lake Hotel, the Deline Dene Band or and the Government of the Northwest Territories Renewable Resources Officer in Deline can generally find Morris for you.

Despite its modern isolation, traditionally, the Johnny Hoe River was the site of a sustained Native subsistence fishery. The Dene fished the spring walleye and fall whitefish runs at

Johnny Hoe for hundreds, if not thousands, of years. When the Second Franklin Expedition wintered at Deline during 1825 and 1826, the Dogrib Indians living near Johnny Hoe sent beguiling messages to the fort about how well they were living. Slavey elders from Deline still talk about camping along the north side of the river across from the Dogrib who camped along the south shore. Both groups built fish weirs in the same ripples. A mile or so from the mouth, several families from Deline maintain an outpost camp for hunting and trapping.

Sitting on the bank of the Johnny Hoe River, in front of Peter Baton's cabin, listening to him talk about all of the people who used to live near the river, the empty woods seem to fill with the shadows of Johnny Hoe and his sons Tachehdue' and Yed'dza. Before he quietly died as a very old man, Tachehdue' told people he would always be near the river if they needed him. People still leave remembrances on his grave.

Once old women sat twisting willow bark into twine for nets where we chatted. Their daughters would have been cleaning fish for the smokers while the men cleared the weirs in the ripples. It would have been a noisy, happy time at Johnny Hoe. Now a discarded fish net, hanging in the tree next to us, quietly reminded us of those times. In spite of the river's human heritage, on an early spring day you and your guide will undoubtedly be alone amid thousands of square miles of primeval boreal forest.

The influence of the Johnny Hoe's warmer water has created a micro-climate at the base of McVicar Arm that is milder than the rest of frigid Great Bear Lake. Bars of re-deposited glacial

sand have formed bars off the river that warm the lake during the long days of summer. It is the only place on Great Bear Lake I have ever taken a comfortable swim.

During spring runoff it is fairly easy for boats to move up the river. By mid-July it is often difficult for an 18-foot aluminum skiff to even reach the outpost camp. When this happens the only way to fish Lac Ste. Therese and the upper Johnny Hoe River is to float down in a canoe. Even at low water, the river is still a couple of hundred feet wide. At lower levels the Johnny Hoe River can be comfortably waded. Where wading is impractical near the mouth, it can be covered from an anchored skiff.

Walleye spawn in the brief period after the river breaks up, but when there is still ice on the lakes. The males come out from under the lake ice when the mouth of the river clears. The water temperature is around 34 degrees F. They are followed shortly by the females. Spawning commences when the water temperatures reach between 44 degrees and 48 degrees F.

My ex-walleye tournament fishing friend Craig Scott was surprised that the northern fish spawn earlier than those in the lower 48 states. Midwestern walleye fishermen expect the fish on the bed when the water temperatures are in the low 50s.

Unless you arrive by snowmobile or helicopter, you will be fishing on the Johnny Hoe River in the wake of the spawn as the fish feed to makeup for a long winter under the ice. The best fishing is probably in late June. At that time, however, the only way in will be by float plane, as parts of Great Bear Lake will still be choked with ice. This is not a problem. There are still lots of fish after the ice clears in early July.

When I was at Johnny Hoe in mid-July, we fished the river down from the outpost camp to the mouth. Although I was consistently out-fished by Tony Tatti with spinners and spoons, my fly rod was not a fish out of water. At first I could not find the right fly. I eventually turned the trick by working the bottom of a deep channel with a sinking line and a size 12 Green and White Clouser nine spine stickleback in line above a size 4 Sculpin. The jig-like action of the Clouser turned the trick. I had similar results with a Brown and Yellow Clouser. Fortunately, Tony was delighted to hang around and offer helpful advise until I hit the right combination. If it sounds like I initial-ly had a hard time keying onto the fish, you're right. Perhaps the reason the fly fishing literature is not choked with advice on catching walleye on flies is because you are generally forced to fish formations in relatively deep water with heavy flies.

Years ago, on northern Manitoba's Hayes River, I occasionally took small walleye on a fly rod with a yellow sally jig. My results were never consis-tent as I was simply dabbling around creek mouths in the spring. Back then, if I really wanted fish I broke out the spinning rod. At Johnny Hoe I was determined to take walleye on a fly rod. Perhaps it was not an accident that I waited to make the big push until I was on world class water with first rate walleye fishermen for whom fish forestalled freeze-dried rations. What I learned is that any good streamer fisherman who is willing to work bottom structures from 5 to 20 feet down has a shot. Your casting will not always be elegant as you turn over a heavy sinking line with a pair of weighted streamers, but the rig is effective. The best flies at Johnny Hoe look amazingly like small jigs.

Although two- to four-pound walleye would have been a gas on my 6 weight rod, I resorted to a nine-1/2-foot, 8 weight that throws a nice open loop in deference to the heft of the flies.

Walleye are carnivores with a cap-ital C. They prey almost exclusively on small fish. The list of potential prey cited by Scott and Crossman in Freshwater Fishes of Canada is nearly encyclopedic in length. If it is smaller than the walleye and swims, it is food. Knowing this, I went armed with weighted streamers that matched the indigenous nine spine stickleback, flat headed sculpin, and smelt or herring. These were backed up by a variety of attractor patterns. In the end, it was imitations of local bait fish based on the Clouser minnow pattern that were the most effective.

Despite my success, walleye are not a natural fly rod fish. Unlike north-ern pike which will readily strike near the surface, the walleye normally must be dredged up from the deep. Given the choice of catching a couple of wall-eye in a morning, or a boat load of northern pike, there is no choice, wall-eye make a better shore lunch.

In most of North America, fly rod-ding for walleye is not high on many peoples' list as warm water tempera-tures drive the fish down shortly after they spawn. In the Mackenzie River drainage of the western NWT, howev-er, there is a window of opportunity in late spring and early summer when the fish are within the range of the streamer fisherman. Since I fished the Johnny Hoe, I have made it my busi-ness to seek out other fly rod walleye opportunities that are easier to access. The key is to stalk them in a riverine situation before they drop back into a lake and go deep.

The Johnny Hoe River can be difficult to hit right. By the time the ice clears in Great Bear Lake and the lodges open later in July, it is really too late for the Johnny Hoe. One northern lodge owner, quipped at me as I prepared this manuscript, "Don't mention Johnny Hoe. It is simply too far away." In a real sense he is right, there are other superb walleye holes that are not overfished and easier to access. Flying out of Hay River, Yellowknife and Fort Simpson there are great opportunities. Trout Lake Lodge and Deegahni Lake Camp, south of Great Slave Lake are, for instance, fly-in operations that open in early June on superb water at a fine time for the streamer fisherman looking for walleye. If you can catch the walleye on the bug, then someday there is Johnny Hoe.

The old village along Johnny Hoe River.

Chapter Sixteen

Travel In The Real Northern Rockies

The peaks of the northern cordillera are not as high as their southern Canadian cousins in Banff and Jasper National Parks, or the towering 14s of Colorado, but they have a grandeur and mystery about them that I find more appealing. Every time I travel in the Mackenzie Mountains, I am overwhelmed by a sense of the unknown.

Eleven to twelve thousand years ago, the valley glaciers of the Mackenzie Mountains separated from the massive Laurentide ice sheet which covered much of northern North America at the time. The torrents of melted water that flowed between the retreating ice sheets awoke ancient drainages and carved new ones around frozen obstacles. Lakes formed behind mountains of glacial debris in barren alpine valleys. As the land rose and shifted following its release from a mile of ice, the water courses continued to move. Huge lakes, once trapped between the retreating sheets of ice, subsided as new channels to the lowlands opened. Shortly after, 10,000 years ago, the Mackenzie River and its tributaries, on the east slope of the Mackenzie Mountains, assumed a northerly flow into the Arctic Ocean.

Amid this turmoil of shifting channels and rising and falling lakes, barriers to fish migration gradually disappeared. Lake trout, whitefish, bull trout, Arctic grayling, and suckers ascended the streams to the high country. Fish probably re-colonized the region around the same time the earliest human populations followed herds of bison, caribou and mammoth from the north coast of the Yukon and Alaska onto the east slope. Fish and humans have had the same amount of time to adapt to life in the Mackenzie Mountains. Instead of millions of years of evolution, we are considering but 10 millennia, a figure that is almost fathomable to our finite minds.

At a misty moment at the close of the last ice age, about 12,000 years ago, archaeologists believe the ancestors of many of North America's Native people slipped across the spine of the Continental Divide from the north slope of the Yukon, and worked their way down the Mackenzie Mountains to the northern plains. Despite the fact that there is a sketchy map in the front of every textbook on North American archaeology showing the proposed route, we know almost nothing of their passage. Some geneticists believe that this first migration was so small that it may have contained as few as three women, who became the "ancient" mothers of Native people in North America! The South Nahanni, Natla/Keele, Mountain and Arctic Red rivers all bisect the proposed "ice-free corridor" route we believe the first Americans followed into the lower continent. I would hate to count the hours I have spent looking for clues along the valleys of the central Mackenzie Mountains, west of Norman Wells, and on the T'logotsho Plateau, south of Nahanni National Park. If your trip passes this way, it is hard not to notice and be curious about the glaciated landscape.

When the naturalist Robert Kennicott crossed the northern cordillera in the early 1860s, he commented on the differences between the lake trout of the Mackenzie Lowlands and the trout of the mountain rivers. The trout he collected from the mountain torrents were probably Dolly Varden bull trout. These were gathered only four years after the first bull trout was collected by G. Suckley and described by C. F. Girard. The species was named Salmo spectabilis after examining the head of a bull trout and the skin of a Pacific salmon! It was later recognized as a charr and then long considered an inland variety of the Dolly Varden Salvelinus malma malma (Walbaum). It has finally been recognized as a separate species Salvelinus confluentus (Suckley). To the Mountain Dene of the northern cordillera, however, it is still simply a river trout.

How have fish and man done in the near Arctic alpine country? Small and tough populations of both have prospered, but neither have been as prolific as their relatives who live at lower elevations and latitudes.

Picking one of the mountain rivers to fish combines angling with white water paddling and scenery that the English language is, at best, inadequate to describe. A mountain canoe trip combines the best aspects of the mountains, boreal forest, and Barren Lands. Starting at the edge of the alpine tundra in a headwater lake, you paddle down through the forested river valleys across a range of Arctic and subarctic cordilleran landscapes to the Mackenzie River valley.

The other advantage to a mountain trip is time. Depending upon your schedule, you can paddle a mountain river with a guide in three weeks. That is a comfortable amount of time to go down the South Nahanni, Keele, Mountain, or Arctic Red rivers. With the exception of the Nahanni, where travel is restricted to canoes, river guides out of Inuvik, Fort Good Hope, Norman Wells and Fort Norman offer jet boat packages. Their speed would let you plan a 5- to 10-day package. Whichever way you choose, the accommodations will be rustic tent camps.

There is a wonderful, arduous, overnight hike from the Keele River to the headwaters of the south branch of Trout Creek where from the top of a terminal moraine you can see both glaciated and unglaciated terrain. You will have to line your canoe up the Twitya River from the Keele River to the mouth of Trout Creek and then hike upstream. Several miles up the creek, you will encounter the boulder strewn remains of the Canol Road. The massive glacial erratics that totally obliterate the old road bed in many places, give some clue to the awesome forces of spring runoff on this normally mild mannered creek. Trout Creek has bisected the glacial moraine, leaving visible fragments on either valley wall that look like a breached dam. At one time after the ice retreated, I suspect the moraine formed a small lake. When you stand on top of it and look up Trout Creek today, you can see a classic U-shaped glaciated valley. When you look downstream, you can see the steep slopes of the V that characterize unglaciated terrain. Although this location is not the key to unlocking the secret of human migration into

The Upper Rampart on the Mackenzie River Near Fort Good Hope.

North America, it is an interesting walk into glacial history and a chance to see one of the roughest sections of the U.S. Army's Canol Road. During the summer, fishing is best around the mouth of the creek.

The Government of the Northwest Territories wants to turn the Canol Road into a hiking trail. If you can hack the Twitya River crossing and the Trout Creek valley, hiking the rest of the Canol is a pleasant experience.

If you want a river without jet boats, the South Nahanni River would be a good choice. Beyond the lack of motors, the Nahanni is a unique mountain landscape. Part of the park was in a glacial refugium, located in the Nahanni during the late Pleistocene, that has not been glaciated for approximately 130,000 years. Our best clue to date on the movement of early human populations, comes from the south edge of the refugium on the T'logotsho Plateau. A warden from the Canadian Park Service, found the base of a Clovis spear point that is at least 11,000 or 12,000 years old. I spent a week working on the site years ago for the Prince of Wales Northern Heritage Centre, but we could not find any other distinctive evidence of an ice age occupation.

The Nahanni's unique glacial history, karst topography, and Virginia Falls, all contributed to the parks selection as a UNESCO World Heritage Site.

Like trips in the other parts of the NWT, you will undoubtedly see caribou, moose, and grizzly bear in the Mackenzie Mountains, but it is the only place you will find Dall's sheep. If you select a South Nahanni River trip that starts high on the river, you might see some mountain goats.

Fishing on the South Nahanni River is better high on the river. You will want a trip that starts at the Moose Ponds or at Rabbit Kettle Lake.

I remember watching a bald eagle grab a fish from a creek near the Keele River. It caught a thermal and soared away over the peaks with a grayling in its talons. Remember a small pair of binoculars.

If you can get on the water in late June, you will catch the spring wildflowers. There will be yellow arnicas in sunny patches and blue backed anemones near retreating snow banks on the upper slopes. There is nothing nicer than finding avens on a flat next to the river when you land the canoe for lunch. Whoever picked the mountain avens as the official flower of the NWT was inspired.

One August day a few years ago, George Pellissey and I sat and ate so many blueberries at the old Shell airstrip at Caribou Flats along the Keele River, that George's wife Vivian speculated we would turn into a couple of old bears.

It is challenging to find the right channel among the braided gravel bars of a mountain river. At night, you can hear the rocks bouncing downstream, swept along by the relentless current. Paddling a braided stream is certainly different then navigating in the more stable channels of the forest rivers on the Canadian Shield or the open Barren Lands. After grinding my way over more bars than I care to remember in the mountains, I was amazed when I travelled with George Pellissey, a Mountain Dene from Fort Norman. We went up the Keele River in a 28-foot scow and never touched the prop on a rock! Reading the water is a fine art in braided channels.

The Arctic Red might be a really interesting trip. I have never been on the river but, I have always been curious about it. The river rises near the Yukon border in a cluster of glaciated peaks that sends streams in four directions. When I was at the PWNHC, we had a report from a man in Inuvik who claimed to have found a mammoth tusk sticking out of the river bank.

Years ago, when I was working in Fort Good Hope, biologist Bob Ruttan told me a wonderful story about coming down part of the river. Bob and Norbert Caesar from Fort Good Hope, were doing a study on marten in the headwaters of the Rampart River. (The Rampart is a small river which flows into the Mackenzie River immediately about the Rampart Rapids.) They had two of Peter Mountain's 12-foot ratting canoes with them that they were using to negotiate the headwaters of the Rampart River. For a reason that I can only presume was wanderlust, they decided to carry their canoes across the low mountain pass between the Rampart and the Arctic Red rivers to come down the Red.

Peter Mountain's ratting canoes are in a class by themselves. They have a slightly wider beam and more rocker than most Dene hunting canoes. Bob maintains that in the hands of a master paddler like Norbert, you can spin one on top of a standing wave and paddle up a rapids like a kayak.

Buoyed by confidence in their boats, they headed down the Arctic Red River. Norbert knew the way so he was able to guide them around most of the heavy white water. When they got to the last big rapids before the river comes out of the mountains, Norbert told Bob to wait while he went to scout it. As he left, he muttered something to the effect that if he did not return shortly, Bob should follow him through. When Norbert did not reappear, Bob started down. Almost as soon as Bob was committed to the run, he ran into Norbert paddling back upriver, frantically trying to wave him off. Unfortunately for Bob, he was not a ratting canoe virtuoso like Norbert and could not spin his canoe on a wave. According to Bob, in shocked disbelief, he discovered that he was being sucked into the flow which flings itself against the cliff at the apex of the bend. The current hits the wall and curls over on itself as it sweeps to river left. Unfortunately, the drama of the attempts he made to ferry to river left, and the flurry of paddle braces

Bob used when he realized he was going to ride the big wave, can only truly be appreciated when he tells the story. The vision of Bob's eyes bugging, his arms flapping, and his head tilting to pull the canoe around the bend still brings a smile to my face. In horror, he rode the left edge of the curl and kept his canoe away from the cliff. At the bottom, he eddied out and in delayed panic waited for Norbert. He waited and waited. Finally a sheepish Norbert appeared out of the mist. When he paddled alongside Bob, Norbert, in his typically understated manner, allowed as how he had never seen anyone ride the big wave.

After you emerge from the mountains, the river passes a wonderful old enclave known as Martin House, where a free trader once had a store. Martin House is located in one of those micro-climatic niches that are scattered around the northern forest, where it always seems a little warmer and the trees grow larger. The Gwich'in land claim has placed restrictions on camping along parts of the Arctic Red. Martin House, for instance, now belongs to the Gwich'in land claim settlement area. If you are on your own and want to camp, you should check with the Gwich'in administration at the address I have given in the last chapter of this book. Your best bet however, is to go with a Gwich'in guide from the community of Arctic Red River and avoid Bob's experience.

Fishing the alpine lakes of the Mackenzie Mountains is one of my favourite experiences. Getting to the lakes is, with the exception of Drum Lake, more difficult than accompanying a canoeing outfitter on one of the mountain rivers.

Chapter Seventeen

Tales of an Alpine Lake

"A light boat, a pair of 30-horse kickers, lots of gas and a little food, that is the only way to climb the Redstone and Moose Horn rivers by boat." Obliquely, George Pellissey and Gabe Etchinelle had just asked me if I wanted to go along on the 150-mile trip to deliver a new aluminum skiff to Drum Lake Lodge. The boat was too big to fly in strapped onto a float plane. When I said yes, George smiled and replied, "By the way, you can only bring a sleeping bag, a sweater and rain gear." Knowing that neither man was famous for packing light, I asked about the river. Gabe replied in his own manner, "When I was a boy, I came down the Redstone River with my daddy in a moose skin boat. One canyon was so bad we had to take the boat apart and carry it around the top. It took us three days. With an outboard on a light boat, maybe there will be no problems." Neither man had ever tried to take a power boat up the Redstone/Moose Horn rivers to Drum Lake. In fact they did not know anyone who had done it. When I asked George's cousin David Etchinelle about the river, he replied, "No one has ever gone all the way up, if anyone can it's George and Gabe." Sitting on the bank of the Mackenzie River in Fort Norman, on a warm summer day, it did not seem that the Redstone could be all that bad.

After poling the boat over a bar from the Mackenzie River into the mouth of the Redstone River, the first day had gone well. That night as we set camp at the hairpin, I thought, "This is a piece of cake". I caught a few Arctic grayling on a Partridge and Orange to supplement our meager rations of bannock and tea. George speculated about taking a Dall's sheep the next day to spruce up our food supply. There is nothing better in the world than mountain sheep ribs roasted over an open fire. I knew there was a reason I liked travelling with guys who carried general hunting licenses. We fell asleep listening to the river rumble around the bend.

Being an observer, I got to watch the rock walls and stunted spruce of the Canyon Range slip by the next day, as George and Gabe navigated. I believe it is an old Mountain Dene axiom that whitemen can not read white water. Actually my job was to look for Dall's sheep while George and Gabe paid attention to the river. When we stopped to build our mid-morning tea fire, I noticed both men were quiet. I mistook their apprehension for being tired and dawdled off with my rod to catch a snack. When we pushed off again, Gabe told me to get my camera ready, he wanted a picture of the next canyon. As we entered, the boils swelled around us. The further we went, the tighter it got. Behind me, George fought the tiller in an effort to follow his uncle Gabe's directions as he pointed the way through the swirling currents. Once past the apex of the S-bend in the gorge, the channel widened and I dared to look back down the Redstone River and watch it roll off the rock walls as it twisted through two 90-degree turns. George pulled over for a break as soon as we cleared the upper end; I have never seen tea go through three people in less time. Gabe grunted that he had been afraid we would have to drag the boat over the top of canyon. He continued to groan about his trip 60 years ago, when they had to pull a 30-foot moose skin boat apart and carry several tons of meat and fat around this small canyon. My canoeist mentality made a mental note, if I ever paddle this river—portage.

A few hours later we branched off into the mouth of the Moose Horn River. The lower Moose Horn is punctuated by nearly continuous class 2 and scattered small class 3 rapids. George confidently slipped the boat around the hay stacks as we continued to climb. Gabe was attentive to the river, but not concerned. I was about to snap a picture of a wave when through the viewfinder I saw the cliff behind us which made the size of the standing waves come into perspective. I instinctively slipped the camera back inside my float coat. As the boat moved alongside the wave, the water rose up along the gunwale until it seemed that only the tension of the meniscus kept it from spilling over. Looking back at George, I saw a standing wave towering over the stern. If we slipped back, the outboards would surely flood. With both 30-horse motors running flat out, George was just able to make headway, pulling slowly away from the wave behind, while steadily angling the bow toward shore. I turned back to Gabe as he flung the coiled bow painter at me and yelled, "Jump, don't lose the rope." Moments later the two of us leapt running from the gunwale to an old snag where we cinched the boat to shore. With our weight out of the boat, the bow popped up and George was able to power the 18-foot Lund into the gravel. With the crisis behind, we gingerly untied the boat and lined it over the inside edge of the ledge. George jumped in and started the engines while Gabe and I held the boat. When he was ready, George signaled for us to leap in as he nudged the skiff out into the current. The steep gradient of the river had obscured the change in wave size which in turn hid the ledge. As we left, George casually commented that a flat bottomed hull with a V-shaped bow designed to plane across the surface of lakes will tend to dig into a river current and be held by it. The rounded bow of a river skiff on the other hand, will ride up a wave giving the operator a lot of maneuverability. No one spoke of the incident again. After we delivered the boat to Drum Lake, it would not have to run the heavy white water again.

At our next tea fire, George busied himself pouring the dregs from all the gas cans into the 10-gallon keg that was feeding both outboards. I did not want to ask how far it was to the fuel cache that was to have been left for us. Fortunately, a few Arctic grayling smoked on green willow improved everyone's mood and we set off on an optimistic note.

An hour later, I was balancing the nearly empty drum on my knee so that the siphons could suck the last gas from the tank. It was obvious we were past the agreed drop, but sometimes you don't ask more than George's looks imply. I glanced at the canyon walls and wondered if the H-F radio would push a signal out of the canyon to the lodge. My speculation was broken by a yell from Gabe. There were three brightly flagged jerry cans sitting on a sand bar. When I jumped ashore to grab them, I was startled by the skid marks of a helicopter's landing gear. Our day had a new mystery.

A few minutes later, as we crawled up through the willow lined channel that was cut when the Moose Horn River drained glacial Lake Drum millennia ago, I glanced back at the Canyon Range. George smiled and pointed down to a peak in the distance and murmured we camped below there last night. We had climbed the Canyon Range by boat. George had not once dinged the propellers on a single rock.

Emerging from the shadows of that last small canyon, the river transformed itself into a broad, shallow and meandering flow picking its way across the ancient bed of glacial Lake Drum. Skirting sand bars, we headed for the Drum Lake outlet. A few minutes later as we emerged from the creek onto Drum Lake, we broke from forest shadow into the orange glow of a midsummer's night. I sighed with relief. It had taken 19 hours of running to cover 150 miles. I could see the ripples of rising trout and Arctic grayling on the lake, but I was too exhausted to restring my rod.

Paul Wright met us at the Drum Lake Lodge dock with a steaming kettle of hot tea. He joked with Gabe about arriving at the Mountain Dene retirement home. In their youth, when he and Gabe had followed the herds, the elders spent their summers at the lake fishing while the young hunters went into the high country after Dall's sheep. The mountain people are adaptable. Now that Paul is an elder, he and his family summer at Drum Lake Lodge, giving sport fishermen a chance to ply these peak ringed waters.

No one mentioned the gas drop until months later, when Lois Hill at Canadian Helicopter told me she had dropped fuel for us when she heard that the guides from the lodge had not made it down the river. She knew George would make it upriver and need the extra gas.

Drum Lake is the largest alpine lake in the Mackenzie Mountains. Situated in the Canyon Range along the front of the cordillera, the lake is tucked in the foothills, east of the craggy Backbone Range, which form the Continental Divide. Drum Lake was born from a blockage in the Moose Horn River at the end of the last ice age. During the late Pleistocene, the river flowed through the lake, spilling out to the east over a wide pass, now 400 feet above the modern lake. It then rejoined the modern Redstone at the hairpin. Later, the Moose Horn eroded a new channel to the southeast through the Canyon Range, leaving a smaller Drum Lake off the main channel. The late Pleistocene drop in lake level probably resembled the draining of a badly cracked bathtub squirting down a steep backstairs. Later, the rate of decline slowed and the modern landscape evolved. Lake trout, Arctic grayling, bull trout, and suckers spread up the Redstone and Moose Horn rivers sometime after the change of course.

Twelve hundred and fifty years ago, the eruption of the White River volcano hundreds of miles to the west in the Yukon Territory, covered the land around Drum Lake with ash. The lake has dropped another 40 feet (13 m) since that time.

The ancient raised beaches around Drum Lake are visible from a plane circling to land at the lodge. If you stand on a hill facing southwest across from the outlet and follow the 2500 foot contour which approximates the maximum size of a lake at the end of the Pleistocene you can see the basin of the enormous lake that once covered the huge wetland that spreads up the Moose Horn River from Drum Lake. I have always assumed that, as a result of the draining of the bigger lake, there should also be some good fishing in some of the deeper muskeg lakes toward the river. It is a theory I hope to checkout one day. On a day trip up the Moose Horn River, to fish a few creeks and look for Dall's sheep, one passes through the old lake bed. There are often moose and waterfowl in the back channels and muskeg ponds. A camera with a zoom lens is in order. The more recent natural history of this dynamic lake is within the memory of Mountain Dene oral traditions. Gabe Etchinelle recalls when he had trouble snaking a small canoe through the outlet. Now an 18-foot aluminum boat with a 30-horse kicker can roar down to the Moose Horn River. Paul Wright likes to point to the remains of a hunter's log raft, sitting in front of the lodge on a raised beach that he remembers as the active shoreline 70 years ago.

Fortunately, the remaining lake is deep enough to provide good fishing until the onset of the next glacial age. Today, the outlet is one of the best fisheries on the lake.

Anglers often rate Arctic fish in terms of the 69-pound record lake trout taken from Great Bear Lake or the 27-pound Arctic char pulled from the Tree River. Sports who have come to Drum Lake to troll for lake trout have not been disappointed, but over the long term Arctic/alpine lakes are not prolific enough to support a fishery designed only to seek the largest fish in the lake. What Drum Lake does offer however, is great fly fishing for Arctic grayling, punctuated by the wild excitement of the occasional larger lake trout or Dolly Varden on a light tippet. I will never forget the 12-pound lake trout I took in the outlet of Drum Lake, on a 8 weight rod and a size 12 Muddler Marabou streamer. At that time, it was the largest fish I had ever taken on a fly rod. Despite the passing of years and numerous much larger king salmon, the memory of that fight is still as clear as the day it happened.

When I first went to Drum Lake in 1985, its potential for fly fishing was largely unexplored. I brought along a pair of rods, an 8 and a 5 weight, because I always carried them, but I had no expectations other than using them as an evening diversion from long days of archaeological survey. My crew left me alone when I went fishing for fear of being garroted by my backcast. In those days, fly fishing was still a carry over from my youth that I continued to play at as an adult. I picked up Arctic grayling for lunch but had not really cracked the secrets of lake trout. Much to my wife Nancy's regret, the two summers at Drum Lake turned me into a fly fishing fanatic.

Rising fish and good water alone do not make a fly fisherman. In my case, it took consistent hatches, the muse of my father's departed friend Bob Harter's fly tackle, and the fish sense of my longtime companion George Pellissey.

After Bob's death, his father Stockton occasionally gave me a piece of Bob's gear when I went to visit and talk about western New York streams that Stockton remembered from his youth. A model 1496 1/2 Pflueger

Medallist loaded with silk line and the most precise hackle pliers I have ever seen became heirlooms. For years, I did not fish the reel because I could not bring myself to change the old silk line. The hackle pliers were carefully guarded from the prying fingers of friends against a day when I believed I would start tying flies. After Stockton passed on, his wife Helen gave Bob's tackle box full of flies to my father. Dad tucked the reel in the box and sent them off to me in the Territories. From the moment I ripped the brown paper off the green plastic box it emanated a need to be used. The following spring, as I packed to go to Drum Lake, I carefully stuffed it in the top of my pack.

Bob's fly clippers replaced the generic toenail snips on my vest. I thought he would be pleased. Later, a box of streamers was tucked into a vest pocket. I continued, however, to resist the old silk line. Finally, one night I dressed the line from a tub of silica I found in his box, and pocketed the reel. The Pflueger balanced one of my graphite rods better then the manufacturer's recommended model. I thought I was able to work a longer line. It felt good, even if people kidded me a little about the line drying over the stove pipe on my wall tent. A few days later, I landed the big lake trout after a 45 minute struggle, using Bob's reel and an old streamer he had tied. A friend's fly was as satisfying to fish my own. I forsook, the palming ring and the tighter drag of my modern reel for the old Pflueger. After that I found myself looking through Bob's Wheatly boxes of dries and old felt-lined leader sinks of streamers more often. The flies were old but they were fishing lures that begged to catch fish and not fall into a drawer vaguely labeled fly collection. Bob

would have wanted them to be used and so I obliged.

I am not sure that George Pellissey really understands why I fly fish. The Mountain Dene are hunters who fish only when they are bored or need food. In the latter case they use a net. Despite his misgivings, George freely shared his intuitive understanding of animal behavior with me in the faith I would become a hunter. I don't believe my shooting disappointed him, but I still prefer my rod to my rifle. George is one of those wonderfully skeptical people who never ceases to question my use of the fly rod as he out fishes me with light spinning tackle. I was therefore delighted one night during our second summer, when he sheepishly admitted, that the heavily weighted Black Woolly Buggers I had given him for his spinning rod had worked well for lake trout. After that George's predatory nature got the better of him and he began to watch insect hatches as he tried to figure out what the fish were eating so he could give me free advice. It is hard to feel you have been one-upped by someone who is instinctively observant of nature. The night when I singularly out caught the other five fishermen in the party, George just smiled and shook his head.

During countless evenings of fishing on Drum Lake, George and Paul Wright showed me the creeks and drop-offs where the Dene had snagged suckers in the spring, set willow bark gill nets for lake trout in the summer, and jigged through the ice in winter. Arctic grayling were taken traditionally, but only really sought in the early spring when they came out from under the lake ice to spawn in the newly opened streams. According to George, although grayling are tasty when freshly caught, they do not preserve well when the flesh is smoked. The Native fishery is predicated on the preservation of food for use later. His retort to my quip about preferring suckers to grayling was apt, they taste better smoked.

As the summer wore on and we recorded numerous traditional fishing camps around the lake, I began to wonder why generations of indigenous subsistence fishery seemed to have less impact on fish stocks then relatively short-term sport fishing and commercial operations. Sport fishing is even having an impact on a system as large as Great Bear Lake. It was a question that nagged me until biologist Fikret Berkes, who has studied the Native subsistence fishery in subarctic Canada, explained to me that the variety of net mesh sizes used by Indian fishers who use what is available, seems to spread the catch out over a variety of year classes. Nor do Natives in the north, target specific species or sizes as much as sports angling for trophies or commercial gill netters who must use specific mesh sizes to meet the needs of processors. Their migratory seasonal round through the Mackenzie Mountains meant that they did not fish the lake every year. The Mountain Dene attitude of not taking more fish than they need helped fill in the rest. They were not trying to catch a limit or meet a quota other then how many dried fish can you carry to your next camp in a dog pack.

The ice goes off Drum Lake in late May. Fishing with caddis nymphs, midges, and black gnats begins to pick up shortly there after. The first good mayfly hatches are evident by mid-June.

Tufted hair Goddard Caddis (sizes 10 to 16), and palmered Bucktail and Elk Hair Caddis (sizes 14 to 18) in olive, black, green, and mottled gray/brown made-up my basic selection of caddis dry flies. Soft hackle partridge and peacock herl, and green, orange, brown and black floss made up my surface and mid-water nymphs. Green Rock Worms in a variety of sizes from 8 to 12 filled out my Drum Lake caddis selection.

My mayfly selection consisted of standard and green floss Adams, light and dark Cahills, Hendrickson's, red and yellow Humpies and Royal Wulffs in sizes 12 to 18. Experience suggests that I should have thrown in a few sized 16 to 22 Blue Winged Olives for early in the season. The use of attractor flies was quite successful. The fish are not subjected to extensive angling pressure and as a result respond well to flies that are the right size and generally the correct colour. My green Adams was tied in response to a brighter green size 16 mayfly that appeared in early July. It was crafted from the meager supply of tying materials I had on hand. A size 16 Blue Quill or a Compara-Dun would be more accurate alternatives to my impromptu fly if you dye the body a more lively green than is used in Blue-Winged Olives. My experience at Drum Lake suggested that Arctic grayling really like flies that sit in the meniscus. The second year, I added parachute variations of my main patterns. Very often the shift from a traditional tie to its corresponding parachute variant worked well when the grayling were being difficult. Gold ribbed Hare's Ears, Zug Bugs and Brown Pheasant Tails in sizes 12 to 18 covered the mayfly nymphs quite well. I got away using partridge and

Tom Andrews fishing in Drum Lake, Mackenzie Mountains.

peacock and brown floss soft hackles as my emergers patterns. Subsequent experience suggests that adding some more suggestive emerger motifs to my Drum Lake assortment would have been profitable. A trailing shuck of white or gray panty hose on a soft hackle fly fished over Arctic grayling is amazing.

A few grasshoppers are fun to have in late July and August. Joe's Hopper, a classic flat water pattern and Chauncy Lively's single-shank hopper for fast water, tied on a size 10 or a size 12 hook, has been as effective as any other pattern for me. In July, I bring along a few tied on size 14 hooks. Variations of greenish-yellow body hues are the coloration's. Because of the short growing season, grasshoppers are not as big in the Territories as they are in more southerly climates. My big hoppers tied on a size 8 hook that are so effective in late summer Colorado, are a waste of time in the NWT. Grayling like hoppers, but hoppers are not prolific at Drum Lake.

Before coming to Drum Lake, I had done most of my Arctic grayling fishing on small tributaries of the Mackenzie River. In rough and tumble pocket water suggestive hair patterns had worked well. Drifting along the drop-offs of Drum Lake in a canoe,

casting to cruising fish required a more gentle presentation. Long leaders and delicate casts were necessary. A slight pause before setting the hook helped relieve the "soft mouth" syndrome. Arctic grayling do not really have soft mouths. It often feels that way to an angler, however, who strikes too quickly at a fish that is simply preparing to take a leisurely bite of the fly. Not surprisingly, dropping a hook size also will help stop short strikes by drawing a more positive response. Flies ranging in size from 14 to 18 are the most successful for Arctic grayling.

Perhaps, it is because the range of the Arctic grayling has contracted so rapidly in the face of civilization, that they have not received their due acclaim as a dry fly fish. Idling in a canoe off Airport Creek one evening, Andy Hammond and I traded the rod back and forth as we alternated catching fish. There were midges, mayflies and caddis on the water. As we experimented with different flies, we both took grayling on flies imitating each of these insects. The fishing was not rapid, but over the course of an evening that stretched through four or five hours of Arctic twilight we caught and released a few fish. When hooked, on each leap the grayling sparkled with different intensities of pink and purple flashes, as they caught the low light of an endless sunset. No records were broken, but then again we were also not skunked. It was an object lesson in good fishing for anyone who believes Arctic grayling are too simple to catch. They are fun but not always easy.

When I got too cocky, George Pellissey would remind me that I was not going to break the 5 pound, 15 ounce Arctic grayling record on Drum Lake. He occasionally prompted me that a three pounder taken off a small creek mouth on a dry fly was a very respectable fish. Reality sunk in and left me eyeing the large rise forms around the lake for what they were, lake trout. Lake trout on a dry fly, hum.

Lake trout and the odd bull trout or Dolly Varden are the other side of the Drum Lake equation. Trolling for lake trout with weighted lines and down riggers represented the first wave of sport fishing on Drum Lake. While it is true that there are very big fish in the depths, there are quite respectable fish plying the waters along the offshore drops. A sinking tip line and a variety of nymphs and streamers bring forth a whole different dimension of fly fishing at Drum Lake. Although I tried a whole range of muddlers, spruce flies and other generic bait fish imitations in sizes 2 to 12, my best results generally came from patterns with pulsating marabou. A slow slightly jerking retrieve that let the marabou wing rhythmically expand and contract seemed to be the key. A basic black or white bodied streamer with a white or yellow marabou wing works as well as anything. Fishing the edge of weed beds near dusk with a golden stonefly, dragonfly, damselfly, or a range of

larger mayfly nymphs is often productive. We regularly took four to eight pound lake trout. My first success at taking small lake trout on dry flies occurred when the fish were up chasing large skating sedges. I plunked a size 10 or 12 Goddard's Caddis near the last rise form and gave it a couple of little twitches. It was a success I have since repeated on other lakes and rivers.

When a few extra lake trout appeared back at the lodge, Mary Rose or her daughter Judith Wright used a traditional Mountain Dene cold smoke to turn them into snacks. Most of the smoked trout was nibbled right off the racks in the teepee as soon as it was ready by folks sitting around an evening fire on spruce bows drinking quantities of camp tea.

For me, the bull trout remained an elusive tale of the fisheries survey that had been done for the lodge. More real, but equally elusive, was the lone chum salmon Paul Wright pulled from his net one day. There is a run up the Mackenzie River that spawns below the Rapids of the Drowned on the Slave River along the NWT/ Alberta border, the fish was certainly a surprise in Drum Lake.

Drum Lake remains a quiet spot tucked in the open spruce forests of the foothill slopes. From the lake, one can see the barren alpine peaks a short distance away. It is off the beaten track from more famous northern waters. The lodge is small and friendly. Charter flights from Norman Wells in the Mackenzie Valley link the lake to scheduled jet service from the south for those who wish to skip the "boat ride". If you want secluded fishing for Arctic grayling and lake trout on a fly rod in a rustic mountain atmosphere it is a good choice.

Chapter Eighteen

A Journal of Fishy Occurrences Near the Canol Road

(June 24—August 6, 1989)

Introduction

The old Canol Road is a corridor for fishing and trekking in the Mackenzie Mountains. It extends from Norman Wells in the Mackenzie Valley to MacMillan Pass on the Continental Divide at the NWT/Yukon border. It is a journey of discovery filled with wild fisheries and occasional barren lakes. There is not a single fish in the place that was introduced by aircraft drop. Perhaps in a way it is like fishing Montana when Montana grayling, Yellowstone cutthroats, bull trout and whitefish were king of the heap, before the decline of the natives and the flood of introductions. All that is lacking from that list are the cutthroats, which in the Mackenzie Mountains are made up for by the sheer quantities of Arctic grayling and the presence of lake trout and Dolly Varden. Three of the four chars available in the NWT are present in the mountains. It is wild too, do not let the term "road" fool you. There are only three ways to travel that so called road—foot, horse and aircraft. Despite this deep wilderness venue, you can drive to the NWT trail head up a rebuilt section of the Canol Road from Ross River, Yukon, or get off a scheduled jet in Norman Wells and take a half of an hour North Wright Air charter.

The Canol Road is a relic of the U.S. armies ill-fated Canadian oil project. Designed to supply the military in Alaska had the Japanese been able to block coastal shipping during the Second World War, the plan was defeated by inhospitable conditions and the U.S. Congress. Military planners proposed to link the oil field at Norman Wells by pipeline and road with the newly constructed Alaskan highway and the coastal defense network. Between 1941 when Arctic explorer Vilhjalmur Stefansson suggested the pipeline and its abandonment in 1944, after a short period of production, the Canol Road remains the only major industrial intrusion to ever cross the Mackenzie Mountains .

Prior to Canol, the only Euro-Canadians that had ever ventured into the Mackenzie Mountains were a few gold seekers during the Klondike rush of 1898, geologic parties, fur traders and intrepid sportsmen. When surveyor Guy Blanchet arrived at Fort Norman in 1942 to pick a route, the path he followed was a series of Mountain Dene dog pack trails. As Blanchet left Fort Norman that winter with his Mountain Dene guide Fred Andrew to map the route to Sheldon Lake, Yukon, he ushered in changes that would alter the world of the Dene forever. Though nature's wrath and the biting questions of men like then U.S. Senator Harry S. Truman ended the Canol Project, the legacy of winter roads and airfields had begun the process of opening the western Canadian Arctic.

Despite the changes it brought, the abandoned road attracted little interest until the growth of back country hiking led the Government of the Northwest Territories to consider redevelopment of the Canol Road as a hiking trail in the early 1980s. I became involved in the process of documenting the traditional history of the Mountain Dene and their ancestors.

I was able to take Blanchet's chief guide Fred Andrew back to Godlin Lake one last time when he was in his 80s. I travelled the Keele River with Gabe Etchinelle and his nephew George Pellissey. Mountain Dene elders Paul Wright and Francis Tatti would call us on the radio at night to suggest new fisheries and mineral licks where we might find Dall's sheep. Perhaps best of all, I was able to walk most of the Canol Road with Tony Tatti as he explored the land where his father Francis had grown-up.

Unlike the old Mountain Dene, we bumped our base camp along the 222-mile trip from Norman Wells to the Yukon border with a helicopter. Our light day packs allowed us to explore huge sections of the mountains near the road without worrying if we had enough beans and rice to make it to Norman Wells. Most fishermen who travel the Canol Road, will follow our lead and fly into specific destinations. To hike the whole road you must travel very light. Those who seek fish should be more selective about their Canol Road destination than the hiker who wishes to travel the whole distance. Although some of the Dall's sheep outfitters will accommodate a few fishermen prior to hunting season, you are generally on your own in a vast wild country. Fishing Canol is still largely an exercise in personal initiative.

A Fisherman's Canol Journal

Saturday June 24, 1989

Today George Pellissey, Tony Tatti, Susan Cross, Susan Irving, and I made a low level helicopter reconnaissance flight along the 222 mile length of Canol Road to check the condition of the road, update our maps and familiarize the crew. The creeks and rivers are high. It is still too early in the season for hikers to ford the treacherous waters of the Twitya and Carcajou rivers. With the snow pack still coming off, even smaller rivers like the Ekwi rise during the day as the melt increases and drop at night when the snow refreezes on the peaks along the divide.

While fishing for Arctic grayling during our lunch break along the Ekwi River, George Pellissey and I reminisced about the time this river almost washed us away. We had crossed the horses through ankle deep water in the morning. After steady rain all day, we had to swim 16 and 17 hand horses back across a stiff current that evening. It was not very hard to convince folks that the small flow we were sitting next to, frequently swelled to fill its broad log strewn gravel flood plain.

Later as we refueled the helicopter at Godlin Lake near Mile 164, the Arctic grayling were rising. Unfortunately, with the weather threatening to close in we did not have time to fish the lake.

On the way home we stopped at Snail Spring (sometimes called Lymnaea Springs) above the Canol Road crossing of the Twitya River. The water is warm but not actually hot. The precipitation of calcareous deposits has formed small dikes that impound large pans of water. Around the edges of the spring, these deposits combined with sphagnum moss to create slightly larger dikes. When we visited, the ravages of a spring flood had left the water flowing through a fairly defined channel. George says more spectacular dikes will form over the summer.

Examining the Twitya River Crossing at Mile 131 from the air, at high water, the only place a hiker would stand a chance of safely crossing the river is near Snail Spring. Above the spring, the force of the current is diffused by a number of braided channels. Below, the Twitya flows in a much more clearly defined bed. The current today was simply too strong to be crossed safely. Winter Lennie from Norman Wells, was swept off his horse while trying to ford the road crossing last season.

About five miles east of Mile 50 on the Canol Road, the Carcajou River drops over two falls and snakes its way through a spectacular narrow canyon. At times the chasm is so tight that we could not see the river below from a helicopter directly overhead.

As we flew down Dodo Canyon past pump station two at Mile 36, George told us the tale of two giants who had a battle behind Echo Canyon. The canyon which juts off the side of Dodo is considered sacred by the Mountain Dene.

Monday June 26, 1989

At 9:00 this morning we tried to fly into Dodo Lakes, nestled in a hanging valley south of Dodo Canyon.

Dodo is an anglicized version of Dall's sheep in Slavey. The canyon is considered a "nest" for sheep by the Mountain Dene, as the animals are protected from wolves by the high crags. The mineral licks along the floor of the upper canyon that give the stream a salty taste are a magnet for caribou, moose and sheep. Whenever ungulates come together, wolves are not far behind.

About 10 km out of Norman Wells, Warren Wright had to turn the Plateus Porter around. There was a small front pushing the ceiling so low that we were in danger of picking spruce cones with the floats. Fortunately, things improved later in the day.

This evening there was a hatch of light brown caddisflies. Though I did not see any fish rising, I tried both an emergent caddis and an Orange and Partridge without success.

Light gray scuds potentially provide another major source of fish food in the lake. Their massive numbers were my first indication that there might not be fish in Dodo Lakes.

Along shore, small black stonefly nymphs were crawling up the willows. Nice bugs, it would be nicer if there were fish.

George and I were quite impressed with the Dodo Lakes. The ground around the upper lake is flat enough for a chopper, easily serviced by a float plane and normally dry enough to camp. Either the Plateus Porter or a Cessna 185, on floats, can land. It makes a good access point for the Canol Road by allowing you to miss the Carcajou River crossing. The steep slopes along the north and south valley walls are nicely contrasted by more open vistas along the east/west axis. The north wall and the lower valley near Dodo Creek are treed, while most of the south and eastern section is open muskeg. It is a lovely tree lined setting.

An important advantage of camping at Dodo Lakes while exploring the canyon is the availability of freshwater. Below the salt flats on Dodo Creek, the stream is very saline. Flash floods are another important reason to camp away from Dodo Creek. Although the creek was easily forded while we were there, at times Dodo Creek is a raging torrent.

Tuesday June 27, 1989

Today we walked to pump station two at Mile 36. We had difficulty locating a spring to prepare a jug of juice, between the Dodo Lakes' outlet and Echo Creek.

On the way back to camp, we stopped to look at the falls in the lake's outlet stream. While we were admiring the delicate cascade, I saw a small grayling trying to jump the first drop. The fish made it about two feet up the face. Another five feet and it would have been into pocket water. One reason that there are no fish upstream is this barrier in the outlet. The lake outlet cascades down a series of rapids and small falls as it drops 50 feet, from the hanging valley into Dodo Creek.

Finding Arctic grayling in the saline portion of the creek was a real surprise. Encouraged by the efforts of that bold fish, I rigged my fly rod and bounced a size 16 barbless Orange and Partridge off the waterfall. Letting it drift down the plunge pool filled with freshwater from Dodo Lakes, to the current line where it mixes with the saline solution in Dodo Creek, I picked up a strike. Over the next 15 minutes I hooked seven grayling between two and six inches in length. Given their size and the scarcity of fish in this area, I carefully released them all.

If stocking of the lake is ever considered, it should only be done with Dodo Creek Arctic grayling. Planting fish from the creek to the lake, would not alter the genetics of Dodo Creek's population when fish eventually escape from the lake. This is an important consideration, because the Dodo Creek Arctic grayling strain is the only one I know of that has adopted to saltwater conditions. When I asked Dr. James Reist of the Canadian Department of Fisheries and Oceans, he expressed the opinion that this population defies normal biological assumptions about the Arctic graylings' intolerance to saline conditions.

Wednesday June 28, 1989

Early this morning George and I climbed the escarpment west of Dodo Lakes. Despite the 2000+ foot rise in elevation, the ascent is hardly more than a very strenuous hike. With care the scree and rock bands can be avoided.

If I were walking off the Canol Road for a pick up at Dodo Lakes, I would consider leaving the road above Dodo Canyon to follow the high ridges and then drop down to the lake.

On a clear day the drill islands at Norman Wells and Bear Rock by Fort Norman are visible from the slopes of Sugar Loaf Mountain.

Thursday June 29, 1989

Today George and I walked up Dodo Creek from the outlet of Dodo Lakes to the headwaters near Linton Lake.

About a mile above the Dodo Lakes outlet, Dodo Creek passes through a tight S-bend canyon. At the lower end of the constriction, a small stream bursts over the rim into a cascade. Amazingly, the Canol Road bed is preserved along the cliff on the inside of the bend. If a few willows were removed, the surface could be driven on. At times of the year, the road must be under 10 feet of water. An old pole from the Canol phone line is visible on top of the cliffs. Phone wires spanned the gorge until Canadian Helicopters cut them to make the flight path through the valley safer.

Above the canyon, the valley opens on the salt flats. There are caribou, moose, sheep and wolf tracks everywhere. Paul Wright told us that when the Mountain Dene hunted the flats they camped along the river bottom.

The salt clears from Dodo Creek above the flats, below the junction of the Linton Lake outlet, the spring creek and a seasonal melt water channel. Along the spring creek fork, Dodo Creek meanders lazily, flowing through defined tree lined banks. There is a dramatic contrast between the badly braided lower stream, dwarfed by high canyon walls, and the gentler, lightly forested slopes of the upper valley. On the spring creek, undercuts line the banks and the stream is shaded by overhanging aspen and spruce.

The walk across the black spruce flat to Linton Lake is interrupted by several rock avalanche tracks. Many of the trees have mud stains almost two feet up their trunks. The upper valley is obviously often under water during spring breakup.

Linton Lake juts out of a steep narrow valley bounded by high talus slopes. Unlike one's expectation of a "clear deep mountain lake", it is rela-

tively shallow. A recent slide flooded out the forest near the outlet. Linton Lake is a reasonable access to Dodo Canyon for a seasoned mountain pilot in a high performance float plane.

As George and I cut back along the talus on the west side of Linton Lake, we found the source of the spring creek. A strong stream flows steadily from a row of five or six springs concentrated along the base of the scree. Given the number of small Arctic grayling in the salty lower section, one can only assume that the mile or so of sweet headwaters must contain the spawning beds.

On the way home we saw a female caribou on the salt flats. When we approached, she tried to run, but stumbled on a bad leg. George says wolves will often nip a ham string on a mother while they make off with the calf. Later they will come back for the cripple. If we were camped on the high ground near the flats, we could watch the drama late in the evening, when the animals come down for salt.

The cutbanks along the flats contain striking lenses of red and green mineral salts. Away from the streambed, ancient scars left by Canol bulldozers and pans scraping gravel for the road are still visible. The cut marks are a dramatic reminder of how fragile this country is, vegetation removed 50 years ago remains an open cut today.

On the trail back up to camp, an indignant bull caribou played tag with us along the lower end of Dodo Lakes. When we first saw him, he was walking near the creek, he then scampered up toward Sugar Loaf Mountain. Later as we neared camp he descended to within 100 yards of us and watched. At that point, I wished I had his energy.

Friday June 30, 1989

George and I walked to Echo Canyon this morning. It joins Dodo Canyon from the west about a half mile below pump station two.

Along the top of the talus slope on the north side of the canyon, we saw an ewe and two lambs resting. Although quite nervous, the ewe allowed us to walk within 100 metres of her nursery. At that point common sense dictated we should not spook them by trying to cross the creek to the base of the scree. With a decent tele-photo lens I could have taken some wonderful pictures.

I had a vague memory of Perry Linton telling me that there were grayling in Echo Creek. As a result, I put my fly rod in the pack this morning. Casting into a pocket formed by a gravel bar that dammed an undercut in a 600-foot vertical rock cliff, I tied into a nice eight-inch grayling. That fish was the only one I landed in Echo Canyon, but I lifted my fly several more times when small fish followed it in the pocket below the second bend.

Echo Canyon is breathtaking. At the top, the gorge is only a few yards wide. Erosion has cut the base out to a width of 10 to 20 yards giving the optical impression of half of an hourglass. The vertical effect of the 600+ foot cliffs looming up to a sliver of light is immediate.

Caution should be used in exploring Echo Canyon. During rainy periods it would be easy to be caught by rising water. Frost action has left much of the rock relatively unstable. If you decide to explore, you should have a hard hat or climbing helmet to protect your head from the continuous rain of falling pebbles.

The surge from Echo Creek nearly doubles the water volume of Dodo Creek. Because the water is fresh, it is a good lunch stop and would make a pleasant overnight camp if you had a primus stove with you. There is no wood in this part of the valley bottom. During a rainy year one would have to watch the weather to avoid being trapped.

After a quick lunch of cheese and pilot biscuits, George and I climbed a steep draw about a quarter mile below Echo Canyon. The gully is one of the few breaks in the lower canyon walls that allows egress to the top of Dodo Canyon.

On our way back to camp, I set up the fly rod and fished the runs and pools in Dodo Creek. Dead-drifting both a Brown and Partridge, I took several grayling between seven and eight inches and attracted strikes from a score of smaller fish. The size of the fish in Dodo Creek dictates fishing with barbless hooks and carefully practicing catch and release. Given a modicum of respect for a limited resource, the fishing in Dodo on very light tackle is amusing. It is not, however, a way to supplement your lagging food supply.

This evening, the clear sunny weather of the last week faded into rain. Thank heavens we had pitched a 10-foot by 12-foot tarp as well as the dome tent. It was large enough to move around and cook as the light rain became a steady downpour.

Saturday July 1, 1989

We awoke to very heavy rain this morning. The ceiling in the valley was less than 500 feet. By noon the intensity of the storm had subsided to a continuous drizzle. The muskeg in the valley was sodden and interlaced with newly born rivulets. Raingear and rubberboots solved that problem. The north valley wall was, unfortunately, too slippery to ascend to the base of Dodo Mountain.

I spent the day exploring the Dodo Lakes. The water near the grassy shore was alive with freshwater shrimp. As I watched, many of them were shedding their carapaces (shells) and becoming instar prior to secreting new, larger ecto-skeletons. During this transition, the shrimp changed from a brownish/olive drab to a bright translucent gray. Sporadically caddis flies emerged throughout the day. Once their wings dried, they skated across the surface and took off. The willows along shore sheltered hundreds of stone and caddis flies on their branches. The absence of fish in the lake has left an abundance of aquatic insects. Perhaps the freshwater shrimp illustrate one of Canol's greatest charms. When the weather prevents you from taking in the mountain landscape, there are other delicate natural wonders to discover.

Sunday July 2, 1989

After being pinned down by the weather yesterday, we were anticipating the break offered by a day of helicopter survey. Our optimism was tempered however, after radio contact with Sue Cross at Mile 74.5. There was snow and near whiteout conditions at higher elevations. About 10:00 the 206B passed over, headed for Sue's camp. From our last radio report, conditions were still marginal but worth trying. Miraculously, Lois Hill was back at our camp by noon, despite low ceilings that forced her to fly through the valleys around the Plains of Abraham.

Our flight path took us southwest of the Sugar Loaf, to Wolverine Mountain. According to Mountain Dene legend, the Carcajou River is named after this peak.

On the way back to camp, we set down by a small lake to catch a few stunted lake trout for dinner. My size 12 Partridge and Orange, and George's 1/8-ounce, 5 of Diamonds spoon worked equally well. I doubt the anonymous puddle would stand much fishing pressure. The presence of fish in the lake has always puzzled me, given what should be a barrier falls in the outlet stream.

Monday July 3, 1989

It rained heavily all night. Wind driven sheets of water continued to lash our camp this morning. By midday the wind had dropped, but the heavy overcast and drizzle continued. The system finally passed, giving our camp a chance to dry out late in the day. George and I drank coffee and read. The rocks were too slippery to hike up Dodo Mountain.

Tuesday July 4, 1989

This is the 200th anniversary of the U.S. Constitution.

Today we finally made the long-awaited hike to Dodo Mountain. There is a 1000-foot climb to the plateau above Dodo Lakes. Once on top, the amount of caribou signs were amazing.

As with the Sugar Loaf on the opposite side of Dodo Lakes, the Dodo Mountain area is extremely good walking. One can wander for hours over gentle undulations that slip in and out of the tree line. While we did not attempt to climb to the top of Dodo Mountain, it would not be a difficult task for experienced climbers.

It was a hot, clear day. By noon we could see the cumulus gradually building up toward the Continental Divide. By the time we returned to camp early in the evening, the sky had blackened. Halfway through dinner, the wind whipped up and thunder started to rattled in the distance. Mountain weather has a delightful cycle of clear days and stormy evenings. After awhile, one only need glance at the sky to know how long you have to get back to camp before the blow strikes.

Wednesday July 5, 1989

This morning, as we walked toward Dodo Creek, it became obvious that the symptoms George had thought to be heat exhaustion yesterday were in fact heart trouble. We managed to walk slowly back to camp to radio the nurse in Fort Norman. Within an hour Medical Services had North Wright Air's Plateus Porter in to take George to the hospital.

After seven seasons with George, his sudden departure left an unspeakable emptiness. I had a stiff drink and took a walk. This evening I learned they had sent George to Inuvik. After the radio check, I settled back to read a Spy in Winter and drink a little scotch.

Thursday July 6, 1989

When the Porter landed to pick me up this morning, the two Sues jumped out and gave me a friendly hug. I don't mind camping alone, but it would have been nice not to do it under such dreadful circumstances. Perry Linton told me that George had been sent south to the University Hospital in Edmonton. Tony will accompany me to Canol Lake near Mile 59 on the road.

As we did a circuit of Canol Lake, Perry explained that there was no surface outlet. The lake drains through an underground stream.

We camped on the west side near the subterranean outlet. In dry years it is very difficult to get a float plane through the weed beds to shore. The drop-off below the mountain is the best access point. Canol Lake's basin is shaped like a soup bowl, deep in the centre and very shallow around the edge. From the mountain behind camp, you see the topography of the lake expressed in emerald green marshes that frame dark blue water. The contrast of brilliant green and dark blue is gem-like in its rich shades and vivid colours. Large rafts of black ducks bobbing out in the deep water completed the image. Tony's palms were itching for a shotgun.

With an obscure outlet, I begin to wonder if this is another fishless lake? My hopes were further dampened this evening, when a large caddis hatch failed to produce any rises.

Sunday July 9, 1989

After two fishless days we were ready to move on. As the helicopter skimmed overhead, Tony spotted a pair of cow moose in a distant water meadow. Lois Hill hauled our camp to Carcajou Lake on the Little Keele River. We dropped our gear on a bench near the outlet and went off for a day of aerial survey.

The open alpine tundra in the upper Little Keele valley is wonderful country to fly over. Cruising along at

500 feet, one has little trouble seeing every fold in the landscape.

Skirting the edges of a frontal system along the Canyon Range, we climbed a low pass and dropped down to McClure Lake in the headwaters of the Carcajou River. Stan Stevens' Mackenzie Mountain Outfitters have their basecamp on the northeast end of the lake. They have been known to take fishing parties into the lodge prior to the start of hunting season.

The lake is deeply incised into the bottom of a broad glacial valley between the Canyon and Cache Ranges. Its surface was covered with rise forms.

Moving down the east side of the Carcajou River drainage, we cut back over the Canyon Range to Andy Lake at the head of Andy Creek. It is another tributary of the Carcajou River.

Andy Lake is in the middle of a gently sloping valley which is covered with low grasses, dwarf birch and Arctic willow. Unfortunately, Andy Lake appears to be fishless.

Lois Hill and her husband Ken Johns made the hike from Carcajou Lake to Andy Lake and back in a very long day. From the air it looks like an interesting walk. You follow the top of the Little Keele River Canyon to the big falls, then cut inland to the divide which separates Andy from the Little Keele drainage. Personally, I would plan the hike as an overnight event.

The Andy Valley was dressed in the bloom of tundra flowers.

From Andy Creek, Lois gently spiraled the chopper up to clear the peaks along the route back to Carcajou Lake. Skimming over the top of the divide, we dropped down McDermott Creek into the Little Keele drainage.

As we turned out over Carcajou Lake, I could see trout and Arctic grayling rising everywhere.

The helicopter dropped us at our camp amid a gathering storm. Tony and I had just set the dome tent when the rain started. After tarping the rest of the gear, we crawled inside, and ate cheese and chocolate until the storm subsided. Later, we borrowed two-by-fours and joist hangers from a fallen outpost camp to make a frame for our tarp. Talk about an uptown set up, our kitchen looked like a beach cabana!

Trout and grayling had been rising in Carcajou Lake all day long. First there was the helicopter survey, then camp had to be set and finally dinner prepared. As the last washed dish clanged to the rack, I couldn't stand the splash, splash, splash any longer and broke out the rod. The outlet of the lake was a madhouse of insect activity—mayflies and giant stoneflies were circling, spinners falling, and midges proliferating. Oh God! What fly should I use first? No particular hatch dominated the evening. The significant factor seemed to be the pattern ride in the meniscus, that nebulous world between dry flies and emergers. I caught a five-pound lake trout and lots of Arctic grayling in the run immediately below the lake. In the elusive moments after hooking one of the grayling, as its tail walked down the river, I knew again why I liked fishing for them. The brilliant flashes of blues and pinks when they jump in the low light of late evening radiated their nickname "tricolour". Their beauty and the mystique of having to search out these native Northerners in seldom visited places makes them very special fish. The quick rise and aerial tricks of the grayling are contrasted by the hard hit of a bull trout. A bull rose from the bottom of the river, grabbed a Caddis Emerger and returned to its lair in a single swirl. Having fish that behave in such distinctive ways makes angling the Little Keele a series of surprises. I glanced at my watch, it was 12:05, I had lost track of three hours.

Monday July 10, 1989

The south side of Carcajou Lake has a number of interesting limestone karst features including a large hoodoo with a passage eroded through it.

Halfway down the shore, we stopped to examined the remains of an old outfitter's camp tucked away in a small sheltered cove. There are still traces of tent frames and a cold cellar. By this time, it had become so hot, we jumped in the lake before catching a couple of fish for lunch. The cold water shocked some more energy out of us and we were able to continue.

Walking near the shore of the lake we found strand lines of driftwood six to eight feet above the current lake level. Carcajou Lake is too small for a storm to toss debris that high. Further, the consistency of the driftwood around the shore of the lake, suggests a major change in water level. An examination of the lake's origin provides a clue. Carcajou Lake is dammed behind a large alluvial fan that flows out of a side valley below the outlet. The Little Keele River has, over time, cut a channel through the leading edge of the fan. New slides occasionally block the river again and alter the level. Erosion gradually eats away at the fan and the level drops again.

Walking on the south side of Carcajou Lake is hard going. At times, cliffs drop directly into the water making it difficult to follow the shoreline.

Above, the valley floor is covered with muskeg and dense stands of willow and birch. Perhaps Tony and I would have growled less if it had not been so damn hot.

On the way back to camp, a large grizzly bear ambled in front of us. Having come from the general direction of the tents we wondered what would be left of our camp. An hour later, when we stuck our heads through the willows, we found that everything was safe and sound. Amazingly the bear never reappeared. Years later, I overheard Tony retelling the story around a fire during a trip on Great Bear Lake. So much for his, oh-it-is-just-a-bear shrug.

The heat of day did not began to break until about 9 tonight. By 9:30, the dishes were finished so I took off for the river. A size 14 Yellow Elk Hair Caddis, trimmed and floated in the meniscus, brought regular strikes. The fish seemed to be feeding indiscriminately on mayflies, caddis and stoneflies. When action slowed on one pattern, I would try another brownish/yellow variation and the strikes would start again.

I dragged myself from the outlet at 11 p.m., to get some sleep. Tomorrow would be another long day.

Tuesday July 11, 1989

Fishing the endless summer nights, walking, and then fishing again is the pattern of our days.

This morning Tony and I waded the Little Keele. Remarkably, we found a series of gravel bars with shallow water that did not fill our rubber boots. The best ford is along the lower edge of the alluvial fan where the current has not had a chance to erode a deep channel.

The short section of river above the alluvial fan runs within well-defined banks, lined with willows and grasses. Below, the outwash's massive outflow of aggregates has filled the old bed and caused the current to braid among the gravel bars. In the six miles between Carcajou Lake and Mile 74.5 on the Canol Road, the Little Keele becomes a heavily braided mountain river.

It was an easy walk across the alluvial fan to a forested bench about 12 feet above the lake. Walking on the north side of Carcajou Lake is a picnic. The ground is well drained. Tree cover and the undergrowth are relatively open in most places. We traversed the length of the lake on a horse trail a few hundred yards from the lake cliffs. On the north end, across the inlet from the outfitter's camp, steep ravines bisect the high ground. I watched a peregrine falcon tuck into its nest on the side of a gorge.

Below we could see the Mackenzie Mountain Outfitters helio-courier strip along the river. Although I landed there once with Perry Linton, the runway is private and not suitable for inexperienced pilots. A float plane landing on the lake is much easier and can deliver more gear, but is not nearly as exciting.

On our way home we raced a thunderstorm. The extraordinary hot weather had caused a massive cumulous buildup. Tony and I ran ahead of a towering wall of black clouds. Making it to camp with minutes to spare, we quickly piled more rocks on the tent guides and doubled the tarp over the kitchen. Moments later, all hell broke loose. Wind, hail and rain beat our camp. The sleeping dome flattened with each gust. Somehow the poles and seams held as it popped back up after every gust. In five hours, three separate fronts blasted over us. Each new torrent was proceeded by a ominous black crescent of cumulous clouds and the distant rattle of thunder. Under the kitchen fly, Tony and I revved-up the gas stove and made freeze-dried turkey and dumplings. Later, we settled back with a cup of tea and listened to the tent rattle.

When at last the lightning was finally past, I rigged the fly rod. Tonight I used a size 12 Goddard's Caddis, to match some big mottled sedges that were skating down the river. These tufted hair flies were made from a caribou that George had harvested near Drum Lake. Tony calls them my Mackenzie Mountain models. On the first seven casts I hooked five grayling. The largest was around 14 inches. None were under 10 inches. After being drowned several times, that devilish fly drooped in the current and enticed a beautiful four-pound lake trout. Goddard's Caddis is tough, it floats well and attracts fish.

Wednesday July 12, 1989

After a long day climbing low limestone hills looking for flint sources, I was thrilled to soak my feet in the river and look for trout. Despite the attraction of the run immediately below the outlet, I was determined to try new water. Crawling over the rocks, I crept down to the base of the second rapids to fish the large pool. What a lovely piece of water. Dammed by the toe of the alluvial fan, it is the deepest water in this section of the river. Using a bright size 14 Partridge and Green, I fished down and across. The fly drifted along a tongue of current that angled into a rock wall about halfway down the pool. The soft hackle dipped under as it swung into the rock and joined the flotsam and jetsam in the upstream eddy. A fish nipped it from under the foam. That trick netted me several more nice grayling before the fly became firmly snagged on the rock and I was forced to break it off. Unfortunately, it was the only one of an experiment. Next year there will be more of that shade in my box.

At the base of the first rapids, I dead-drifted a caddis larva. Nearly every cast brought action. Later I tried to match the golden stonefly nymphs crawling up the river bank with a size 8 Ted's Stonefly larva. I took several more nice grayling before the fish stopped striking. Who says grayling are not selective feeders? Later they begin to rise for size 20 Midges. Rather than walk back to camp and dig out more flies, I decided to call it an evening and retire.

It was still hot at 10:30 tonight. Tomorrow will be a real scorcher.

Thursday July 13, 1989

Tony and I decided it was too hot to transect when the sun baked us out of our tent at 6:30 in the morning. We dawdled at important jobs, like airing our sleeping bags, washing work pants, and sorting and repacking our food. (Given the frequency of daily showers you cannot leave your sleeping bag hanging out while you are away from camp.) Over the past couple of weeks, extra food has piled up until we are in danger of bulking out the helicopter. I was amazed that our new pile was only half the size of the old one, but then again how many freeze-dried pears can you stomach. Lois will haul the extra food back to Norman Wells.

Our prediction that this would be a hot day was a gross understatement. I half expected to see the film crew for the remake of Lawrence of Arabia ride by on camels. Despite a nice midday hatch, the fish did not rise today as they have for the last week.

It was nine tonight before the heat begin to break. As soon as the temperature dropped, the Arctic grayling started to rise. Tony tried fly fishing for the first time tonight. After watching me, he decided control of the loop was a lot like using a dog whip. The tight loop is essential for both activities. As Tony and I swapped the rod back and forth after each strike or fish, it lent a little friendly competition to the evening.

Joe's Hoppers provided all the action we wanted. Although many of the strikes were slightly short, we caught our fairshare of fish. Next time I tie the pattern, I want to add a touch of green to the yellow body.

Differences in the colour of the lake trout in the Little Carcajou Lake are quite distinctive. Some are pale green, with faint spotting, white bellies, just a touch of white on the tips of the fins and white meat, while others have dark bodies, much stronger square white bars on the fins, golden/amber stomachs, more distinct spots, a touch of pink along the lateral line and red meat. Part of the difference may be diet. For instance, according to Canadian Department of Fisheries and Oceans biologist, George Low, fish that are feeding on scuds will have redder coloration than trout that are keyed in on herring. There may also be different strains of lake trout. Given the size of the lake it surprises me to see so much variation in the fish.

The big news on the radio check tonight was the massive outbreak of new forest fires in the Mackenzie Valley. Smoke from those fires shrouds the eastern horizon.

Towering cumulous have been building to the west all day. I hope the storm passes overnight so that we can fly tomorrow morning.

Friday July 14, 1989

Lois roared in at 9:45 this morning. Tony and I were all packed and ready to move, but where along the Carcajou River should we set our next camp? My original plan had been to set up by the mouth of Andy Creek near the base of the Plains of Abraham. Leon Andrew from Fort Norman told me about a good fishery near the junction of the creek with the Carcajou River. During our over-flight at the start of the survey I had noted that there was a lot of muskeg in this area that would make foot survey difficult. What to do? From Andy Creek, the Canol Road follows the Carcajou River to Bolstead Creek and then climbs over the pass into the Trout Creek drainage. The Canol Road continues down the Trout to the lower Twitya River. We followed the Carcajou River past the turn in the Canol Road at Bolstead Creek, and flew on to McClure Lake. Our wants were simple, high dry ground with easy access to the river and/or the lake. The McClure Valley is a broad glacially-scored U, characterized by very poor drainage above the steep walls of the lake glen. Reluctantly, we decided that unless we camped next to Mackenzie Mountain Outfitters at the far end of McClure Lake, the prospects looked poor in the actual headwaters of the Carcajou River.

Our next choice was pump station 4 four at Mile 108 on the Canol Road. Eight miles up Bolstead Creek from the Carcajou River, Mile 108 offers the opportunity to walk back to the Carcajou River, easy access to the Trout Creek Pass, and close proximity to the country around Mount Eduni. It has the added benefits of being one of our helicopter fuel caches and offers a Quonset hut in which to sleep. Our mountain tent could be hung out to dry in one of the old garages.

After dumping our camp and refueling, we set off to explore. The country around Mount Eduni is simply staggering. Some of the hanging valleys have thousand-foot cliffs beneath them. We stopped to investigate a pair of cirque lakes on the southeast side of the mountain. Unfortunately, they were fishless.

From Mount Eduni we flew east to the Keele River, crossing at the salt outcrop referred to by sheep biologist Norm Simmons as the "Mother-in-law" lick.

Later, after investigating some small lakes, we flew back to the Carcajou drainage via Porter Creek. Porter Creek valley was used by the Mountain Dene as a trail between the Keele and Carcajou rivers. Deceptively, the drainage flows two ways. A small creek that seems to rise on the Keele River side of the Porter Creek moraine, actually flows under it, through an aquifer from the lake on the Porter Creek side. The large flow that springs forth from the Keele River side is startling. As we crested the moraine, there were three moose feeding in the headwaters of Porter Creek.

At our fuel cache high on the Plains of Abraham, we took stock of the day. I wished to continue our aerial investigation along the northeast side of the plains, but it was obvious from the black clouds towering on the western horizon that our time was limited. What the hell, we were flying in a portable rain shelter and our gear was safely stashed inside at Mile 108.

Saturday July 15, 1989

Tony and I reveled in our new-found elbow room. Private suites after weeks of being crowded into a mountain tent. One of the Quonset huts was re-roofed by Economic Development and Tourism for use by visitors.

Pump station 4 is another one of the most scenic spots on the Canol Road. The Bolstead Creek valley separates the Cache Range from the Mount Eduni. This break in the mountains is punctuated by towering rock on either side of the Canol.

Because the helio-courier can land next to the camp, Mile 108 is a prime staging area and resupply point for hikers on the Canol Road. There is very little firewood near Mile 108. It is a wise idea to have a gas stove along.

This morning Tony and I crossed Trout Creek Pass on the Canol Road. The track rises quickly from the Bolstead Creek, hugging the valley wall. With the tree line eight miles behind at the Carcajou River and three miles ahead in Trout Valley, one is surrounded by high alpine tundra. Hiking along a good trail, we were free to look for the divide where the waters of Trout and Bolstead creeks split to feed the Twitya and Carcajou rivers respectively. Below, the old telephone line hung limply from a few poles that remain tenaciously upright. Over the crest of the pass, Trout Creek descends quickly. It has cut a narrow glen into the broad, glaciated valley bottom.

Down the valley, we spotted a large ridge protruding from the west side (circa Mile 113). We climbed it and while sitting on the crest and eating lunch, I casually noted the ridge had once blocked the valley before it had been eroded by the creek. Hum, a nice U-shaped valley above the ridge, and a rather V-shaped valley below. We were sitting on an ancient glacial terminal moraine. At some point in the distant past a valley glacier stopped where we ate.

Despite their name, the headwaters of Trout Creek were not very fishy.

Sunday July 16, 1989

This morning Tony and I took the southwest branch of Bolstead Creek toward its headwaters on Mount Eduni. A few minutes after leaving camp, we met a magnificent bull caribou in velvet. He was totally unafraid of us. In fact, he didn't challenged our passage across his territory. Circling the bull, we began our ascent toward the headwaters of Bolstead Creek. Climbing smaller and steeper tributaries we finally gained the pass between the Carcajou and Keele River drainages. From the pass, we could see a number of sheep trails, but unfortunately, recent high temperatures have sent the sheep to higher, cooler places.

On the way home, we discovered a bed of crystals next to Bolstead Creek. It struck me as odd to see free quartz crystals eroding from a layer of finely crushed black shale. Tony found a couple of real "gems" to take back to his niece.

We crawled up through some very rough country today, barren of vegetation, except for a lush mat of green moss that welcomed us to rest on the pass. Day trips out of Mile 108 onto

Mount Eduni, are spectacular. For experienced hikers, there are breathtaking views, geological exposures and with luck, Dall's sheep.

Monday July 17, 1989

Today we headed down Bolstead Creek to the old road maintenance shop at Mile 100, near the confluence of the creek with the Carcajou River. Broken bits of chain, crawler tracks, and truck parts reminded us of the men who toiled to carve the road toward the Continental Divide 120 miles, to the west.

Coming down the valley from Mile 108, one leaves the canyon and emerges into the broad Carcajou Valley. As the mountains fade on either side, a few scattered trees appear on the tundra, first in the shelter of narrow creek cuts and on the south sides of low hills. Slowly the density increases until one has entered an open pine/spruce forest. There is a striking image of perfectly shaped "Christmas" trees thinly spread across the valley. Over a space of eight miles, one passes from the barren slope of Mount Eduni to the spruce-lined banks of the Carcajou River.

At Mile 106, Tony and I spotted a lone caribou resting on a huge ice pan in Bolstead Creek. It is amazing that with all the hot weather we have had the last several weeks, ice can still exist. A little while later we surprised a cow caribou and a calf at a creek crossing. She studied us briefly as we picked our way across the boulders and then slowly ran off.

By a tributary at Mile 101, a large bull caribou hurried down the slope ahead of us. Without looking, he ran toward us with his head down. Suddenly, he jerked upright, stared

and then bolted to the left. His muzzle frothed from a long run. Tony thought he must have just escaped a wolf.

We ate lunch by the old road maintenance building at Mile 100. Within minutes of our arrival, black clouds that had been looming behind us all morning let loose in a torrent. Smugly, we laid back on the old bunks and took a snooze despite the smell of rancid porcupine pee.

Our original plan had been to continue on to the old Carcajou River bridge. Now with very unsettled weather hanging over us, discretion dictated that we start the eight mile hike home as soon as the storm broke. The fish in the river would have to fend for themselves.

Near Mile 103, a young bull caribou crashed out of the bush and ran down the road toward us. When he was about 60 feet away, he shook his head and jumped back into the trees. This is the second agitated animal we have seen today. There must still be a wolf hunting nearby.

On the way home, we averaged three miles an hour, despite the washouts and slides. It is unusual to be able to consistently walk that fast along the road over an eight-mile distance.

When we crossed the culvert below the pump station 4, Tony noticed three small bull trout holding at the tail of the plunge pool. Given the heavy braiding and shallow water in Bolstead Creek, it is amazing that trout have made their way this far up from the Carcajou River. Although some of the channels in Bolstead Creek have always appeared fishy to me, I have never successfully fished this heavily braided stream. You would need hip boots and gutsy wading shoes to work your way over the lose cobble bottom.

The small branch of Bolstead Creek that skirts behind the pump station and rejoins the main flow through the road culvert where Tony saw the fish is polluted. Above the pump station, we found mayfly, stonefly and midge nymphs. Below an old dump and several oil spills, the main channel is dead. Turning rocks along approximately 200 metres of streambed between the camp and the culvert, we managed to find only one mayfly nymph. There were no stonefly nymphs.

Not only is a potential spawning area endangered by this lingering Canol taint, but the water supply for Canol visitors is jeopardized. There needs to be a cleanup. In the meantime visitors should draw their water from the main channel of Bolstead Creek above the camp.

About 11 tonight the wind and rain returned with a vengeance.

Tuesday July 18, 1989

When I got up during the night, heavy fog had dropped the ceiling to ground zero. It turned into a morning one hoped would go away if you did not get-up and acknowledge it. When hunger finally drove me from bed about 10:00, the ceiling was at 600 feet but the wind was now driving the rain sideways. Knowing our plans to ascend the valleys in the Cache Range behind our camp were in ruins, we began to wonder if the helicopter would make it in tomorrow. With so many rain days, I was now rereading Rick Hafele and Scott Roederer's An Angler's Guide to Aquatic Insects and their Imitations for all North America for the second time this summer. This one little volume is all you need afield in the NWT.

This afternoon, when the deluge softened to mist, Tony and I donned raingear and walked back to the plunge pool to look for the trout. Eighteen hours of rain had raised the little creek six inches. It was now a mere two-inch jump from the plunge pool into the culvert. Neither of us were surprised to find fish above the road crossing. Despite low summer water levels, the little creek has enough spring-fed gravel runs to suggest that it is probably a spawning bed for the bull trout. Perhaps the trout eggs survive because of untainted water from the springs. It would have been fun to see if the fish actually built redds.

Below the camp, streamside vegetation has recovered from the channel being rerouted during Canol construction. Lacking the severe channel braiding found in Bolstead Creek, this flow is concentrated in a relatively narrow bed between stable grassy banks with a few small undercuts. If there were more bugs, it would be the perfect trout stream.

Wednesday July 19, 1989

I awoke chipper as a bird at 4:30 this morning. Somehow I managed to keep myself from springing out of bed until 6:40. Dressing quickly, I dashed out for a half hour walk along the Canol. Poor Tony, I came waltzing back ready for anything.

Lois Hill arrived with a full load of fuel on the 206B to maximize our survey range. Our first task was to check the high valleys and ridges in the Cache Range north of Mile 108 for ancient Mountain Dene sheep fences. Though we traced a number of prominent trails, we failed to find any fences as we worked down Trout Creek and then followed the Twitya River up to Deca Creek. Skipping over the height-of-land to Mountain River drainage, we started down from the headwaters of Abandoned Creek to Cache Creek. We found good fish habitat but did not have time to prove it by fishing.

Crossing a low divide to Cache Lake on the east branch of Cache Creek, we found a charming alpine lake. I could spend a week exploring the lake and climbing the mountain that rises from its waters.

From Cache Lake we flew southeast over the low divide into the west fork of the Trout Creek drainage. Originally, we had planned to camp at the Trout Lake cirque. A brief aerial survey, however, revealed poor drainage that convinced us to move downstream.

We finally set our camp on the Canol Road about a half mile below the junction of the east and west branches of Trout Creek.

The creek flows down a interface between sandstone and shale formations. Large sandstone slabs in the creek below our camp were wonderful places to sit on and contemplate the bubbling water. Despite the promise of fishing by my friend Gabe Ethchinelle in Fort Norman, there were no trout in the rock pools near camp.

Below the confluence, the valley constricts forcing your line of sight to vault skyward to the cathedral spires of rock along the north wall. As the orange light of late evening filtered through the gaps, the crags laid eerie shadows across the valley.

Thursday July 20, 1989

Tony and I walked up the east branch of Trout Creek this morning toward Mile 108. After wading bitterly

cold water and picking our way over boulder fields, we arrived at a small ridge west of the terminal moraine that felt like a good place for lunch.

On the way back we climbed the valley wall to avoid the long ford we had made this morning. On the upper slopes of the valley, we picked up an outfitters' horse trail that paralleled the Canol telephone line. Both the trail and line dropped back down to the creek at the confluence of the east and west forks.

Trout Creek's scenery is one of the gems of Canol. I have never seen a stream with such shimmering, translucent green water. Yet beware, for it is not tame. Massive washouts of the road, huge flood channels, and avalanche shoots are silent reminders of a more violent presence. Remnants of the torrents make walking very hard. The valley bottom is strewn with boulders the size of small houses. Even the best route requires several icy fords of the stream. The worst conditions can be missed, however, by following the horse trail up the east branch until the Road creeps out of the creek bed again. Hiking this section requires extreme care.

All day the cumulus slowly built up in the west. At 7:00 the heavens had opened up. The ceiling dropped and clung to the midriff of the peaks. Over tea we discussed the possibility of a flash flood.

Friday July 21, 1989

Once again Thor treated us to an all-night rain. Foolishly believing it was over, we got up and made breakfast. Without fail, the heavens broke open again. At least it waited until we had finished eating and were getting ready to start walking. The rocks were too slippery for safe travel. With only a few brief respites, it poured heavily all day.

During one break, I ventured downstream to look at the hole formed by the confluence of a tributary. What wonderful pocket water! I cannot understand why there are no fish. Perhaps they only come up here during a spawning run. There were black midges hovering over the back waters. Rolling rocks, I found lots of clinging and crawling mayfly nymphs. A mystery—maybe the pH of the water is wrong, there are not enough wintering sites, or breakup is too harsh. For whatever reason, this gorgeous stream is fishless in late July.

Despite 18 hours of steady rain, Trout Creek has risen very gradually, the clarity of the water has been only slightly tainted. I had been expecting far worse.

Saturday July 22, 1989

Today we went up the west branch toward Trout Lake. The lower slopes were muskeg. When we arrived across from the pass to Deca Creek, there was another long, knee-deep ford through icy water. It was a cold dark day, that was not at all conducive for water sports. I decided that rather than plunging through the creek, we would come back with the chopper.

From here our transect turned inland over the ridges between the east and west branches of the creek. The lower elevations were draped in muskeg, but the ground improved as we climbed. Then, Oh happy days!, we got caught in a real downpour. Thank God work clothes dry quickly. It was simply a prelude of the slippery ford on the way home.

Such a black, miserable day could only be saved by a big pot of freeze-dried chicken and Bisquick dumplings.

Sunday July 23, 1989

Dawned revealed a clear day.

We used the helicopter to move camp to Godlin Lake, near Stan Simpson's (Ram's Head Outfitters) place at Mile 168. We quickly unloaded, refueled the helicopter and flew off to the Bluefish Creek.

Godlin Lakes was one of our best camps of the summer. The two lakes are blue stones in an emerald valley surrounded by craggy peaks.

The mouth of the Bluefish Creek would be a lovely place to stream fish. At that point, the Twitya is a broad, heavily braided river. Flying upstream, we followed the braids to the lower end of the canyon where George Pellissey was born. His mother gave birth as the rest of the family built a moose skin boat to travel down to Fort Norman to trade.

A short distance above George's birth place, we flew over the site of a tragic moose hide boat accident. According to Gabe Etchinelle and Paul Wright, a party of Fort Franklin people had built a boat above the canyon. When they reached the top, the men put the women ashore to walk around the canyon. Moments later, the boat came apart on a ledge. Everyone on board was lost. A party of Fort Norman Mountain Dene found the women camped below the canyon weeks later.

On the way back to Godlin Lakes, we followed the Caribou Cry River upstream from its junction with the Twitya River. Several miles from the mouth, there are some interesting rapids and a small canyon that looks like it would have great fishing. Above the canyon, we cut south to Bluefish Creek and then hoped over the divide to Godlin Lakes.

The evening storm roared through the valley shortly after our arrival, soaking the ground before it fled east. The change in weather was enough to start the grayling rising in the upper lake.

A white grizzly appeared on the mountain behind our camp tonight. I could not tell through the spotting scope if it had the pink eyes of an albino or not.

Monday July 24, 1989

Tony and I walked to Mile 170 on the Canol Road this morning to examine Pump Station 5.

The road from Godlin Lakes to MacMillan Pass has very pleasant scenery, unfortunately the numerous fords can make it difficult to hike if there is high water. I rode part of this section on horseback in 1983. A horse is a wonderful addition to the trip. It lifts you above the nasty little fords and allows you to swim the big Ekwi River in style. This year Wendy Grater and a companion from Black Feather Wilderness Adventures rode from Godlin Lakes to the border on mountain bikes.

A brisk wind put the Arctic grayling down tonight. Godlin Lake may well have the best fishing along the entire Canol Road.

Tuesday July 25, 1989

There was a sporadic rise of grayling to midges on the upper lake this morning. Lying on the dock, I watched a 12-inch grayling drift up from a weed bed to suck midges from the meniscus.

Tony and I followed the Canol Road from the outfitters' camp at Mile 168, down the Godlin valley to the old road crossing of Godlin Creek (circa Mile 163) below the outlet of the lower lake.

Although overgrown, this section of the road is good walking. The ford across Godlin Creek is thigh-deep, through a slow current. Below the lower lake there is excellent bull trout and Arctic grayling fishing.

Today was rotation day for the sheep hunters. We were treated to a small air show as the sports were picked up and dropped off at various outpost camps by Stan Simpson's three Piper Cubs.

This evening grayling fry were chasing skating caddis around the lake. I used a size 12 Skating Caddis to try and discourage the little nippers. I was so busy shaking off small fish that I missed several good strikes.

Wednesday July 26, 1989

Panting from the heat, with a storm threatening, we limped back to camp minutes before the tempest hit. This evening after the blast there were sporadic caddis and midges hatching on the lake. Although the fingerlings went nuts, the larger grayling were quite selective.

Thursday July 27, 1989

While I washed up at the dock this morning, I watched the "troll under the bridge" chase away all the smaller fish. Having reached the exalted size of 16 inches, this old grayling holds the float plane dock as

Fishing the eddy on the Ekwi River, Mackenzie Mountains.

his own private sunshade. Tony and I both sat and watched him defend his turf for a few minutes before breakfast.

Later, we walked over the low divide to a small canyon that drains into the Ekwi River below pump station 5. The creek has two forks. One rises on the south side of Mount Burrell, crossing the Canol Road at Mile 170. The second drains the area south of the Godlin divide. After a fruitless morning on the flats, we stopped for lunch and caught a couple of Arctic grayling from an undercut cliff on the Ekwi River.

On the way back to camp, we stumbled upon a wonderful spring creek. I caught and released a 17- and an 18-inch grayling on a size 16 Soft Hackle Zug Bug, from undercuts. It is the perfect stream—about a half mile long and less then 20 feet wide, it has an pleasant mix of small pools, brisk runs and even an old beaver dam. Relatively open banks allow carefully placed forward casts to be made. The price for easy casting was a lot of crawling on my knees. I only had to back my butt into the brush and use roll casts a couple of times. Discoveries like this restore your faith in serendipity.

Friday July 28, 1989

After 14 straight hours of heavy rain, we crawled out of our tent at about noon to examine the upper lake.

Pausing to fish in the outlet, we found a score of Arctic grayling laying in the shallows. With a couple of fish in the pack for dinner, we continued on around the lake. The stand of stately spruce around the east shore backs wide water meadow.

The melodic clanging of bear bells on the outfitter's horses cut through the evening mist to break the silence.

Saturday July 29, 1989

This morning Tony and I went down the west side of the upper lake to the outlet. We crossed and followed the creek to the lower lake. The east side of the outlet was quarried for gravel during Canol construction. The scraper tracks are still visible on the ground surface.

We tried to follow the shore around the lower lake but wetlands and steep banks forced us to work our way up to the Canol Road. At the bridge over Godlin Creek, we spread out to see if we could find any fish around the outlet. The ground is quite low and has frequently been flooded by beaver. We spooked some very nice bull trout and then caught a couple of grayling that we roasted on the fire for lunch.

Sunday July 30, 1989

Moving day. North Wright Air called to confirm that the Islander would be in early this afternoon to haul us to Mile 222 below MacMillan Pass. Debbie Simpson kindly loaned us a wheelbarrow to haul our gear up to their airstrip. After the move, she treated us to a hot shower and fresh bread. We thought we had died and gone to heaven.

When the Islander arrived we unloaded the four drums of turbo B we owed Canadian Helicopters and threw our gear on board. We were headed for the border on the last stage of our Canol odyssey.

Jim Hickling, the GNWT Renewable Resources Officer stationed at the border, picked us up at the Mile 222 airstrip in his truck. We stayed close by in the old weather station behind his trailer. The building dates from Canol, but has been recycled several times.

Monday July 31, 1989

Tony and I inspected a series of ridges and eskers on the south side of the T'sichu River today. Walking through the MacMillan Pass area is extremely difficult. The dwarf birch are six feet high. We were both tired when we got back to camp.

Tuesday August 1, 1989

Crossing the river this morning, Tony accidentally kicked a bull trout laying in a shallow riffle. I am not sure who was more surprised, but the fish was certainly upset. The fishing in the T'sichu is not easy, but there are trout if you work the pockets in the large shallow ripples. Soft hackle flies with a single piece of split shot on the nose of the fly worked very well. Upstream from the Canol Road crossing, there are six- to eight-foot tall willows growing in the stream. Talk about angling in the forest. Behind Mile 222, the T'sichu River is about 20 yards wide and one foot deep. Another classic braided stream.

Wednesday August 2, 1989

I fished in the T'sichu this morning. Pheasant Tail Nymphs moved a couple of fish.

Thursday August 3, 1989

While we waited for the plane, we tried fishing in a small creek near MacMillan Pass. It was absolutely dead. The stream had a lot of mineral staining along its banks, the pH may be off for trout.

The plane tried to get in tonight but turned back because of bad weather.

Friday August 4, 1989

Jim Hickling says that many of the hikers coming off the trail are in poor physical condition because they have run out of food. Two hundred and twenty two miles is a long way to walk. If you want to fish, concentrate on one or two sections. It is fun to search the unknown, but there are too many empty lakes and streams to risk your whole trip on a guess. The

Mackenzie Mountains have never been stocked and so there is a lot of promising water in which there are simply no fish. The southern Rockies had similarly spotty fishing until they started to stock the high country lakes.

Saturday August 5, 1989

The Twin Otter came in to pick us up this morning. As we jumped off the plane in Norman Wells, there was a line of camouflage clad hunters loaded down with rifles and fishing rods waiting to fly-in for sheep hunts. A little worse for the wear after a summer in the mountains, several of the sports gave us looks that seemed to say, we had to wait for that big plane to pick you guys up? Have a nice trip folks. It was time for a shower and a beer.

A cirque in the Mackenzie Mountains near the Canol Road.

Chapter Nineteen

With Rod In Hand

People have lived in the NWT for thousands of years and yet you can still go places where you feel like no one has been there before. My old friend George Boots, an 80-year-old Dene trapper from Willowlake River, keeps telling me that his moccasin tracks are "all over the country". George's trails and camps, however, don't leave a big scar behind. I wish more people could appreciate George's philosophy and leave only their foot prints and a few fire cracked rocks in their campfires.

Inuit and Dene hunters who live on the land have a mythical "connection" through their ancient tales with the animals. Their legends teach that the creatures of the land, sea and air give freely of themselves so that the Native people can be sustained. In return, the Inuit and Dene obey rituals that maintain the spirits of the animals guaranteeing that there will always be more game. The traditional oral narratives of northern hunters are more than folk tales. Within the Native stories about creation, encounters with animals, and journeys long past, are encoded the information that allows each new generation to learn their home territories and wander the hinterlands that stretch to the horizons of their world. Around countless winter fires, long paddles, and endless hikes, the elders tell their children and grandchildren how to find game, deal with dangerous animals, and where the trails and rivers lead. Without a

Native hunters survival skills, few can be as cavalier as my friend George Pellissey who declares you are never lost if you do not care where you are.

Lacking this primal connection and life long experience on the land, it is easy for fishermen to misunderstand the seemingly friendly curiosity of wild animals. Without the hunters instinct, many forget that moose, caribou, bears, and wolves can be dangerous. A 900-pound cow moose protecting her calf is a force to be reckoned with.

People often find it is difficult to understand that simply because a snowy owl will permit you to approach its nest, does not mean you should approach it. Arctic foxes will follow a human scent and raid a nest that a person has approached.

The seeming abundance of fish on isolated rivers and lakes, leads many people who would otherwise know better, to think that they are an inexhaustible resource. Convincing them to fish with barbless hooks, so that the excess can be harmlessly released, is a matter of education.

Anyone 16 years or older requires an NWT Fishing License. If you enter the Inuvialuit Settlement area, or fish within the Great Bear Lake fisheries management area, you require an additional stamp on your fishing license. These can be obtained from most sporting goods and hardware stores, the RCMP and NWT Department of Renewable Resources Offices.

Fishermen travelling on parts of the Slave and South Nahanni rivers must also obtain a National Parks fishing permit from either the Nahanni National Park office at P.O. Box 300, Fort Simpson, NWT, X0E 0N0, or the Wood Buffalo National Park office at P.O. Box 750, Fort Smith, NWT, X0E 0P0.

Many fishermen do not realize that if they plan to pass through any of the 16 Migratory Bird Sanctuaries in the Northwest Territories, they must apply to the Canadian Wildlife Service for a permit. The permits allow CWS to limit access during critical nesting periods and to keep track of the number of parties that pass through the sanctuaries. Information and sanctuary permits can be obtained from the Canadian Wildlife Service, Box 637, Yellowknife, NWT, X1A 2N5 (403) 920-8530. Permits take about a month to process.

It surprises me that many fishermen still incorrectly believe that they can carry a rifle and live off the land. Wildlife regulations in the Territories are designed to conserve the resource and prevent waste. Non-residents of the Northwest Territories must be accompanied by a licensed guide to hunt big game. The season for migratory birds does not open until September 1st. By that time most fishermen have finished their trips and departed for the south. Bears may be shot in self-defense or if life or property are threatened. A gun should however, not be your first line of defense

against a bear. A clean camp, keeping food away from sleeping areas, watching for fresh signs and staying clear once you sight a bear, are your best options. Do everything in your power to avoid a confrontation. To kill a charging bear with a rifle you must be able to remove the gun from your shoulder, chamber a round, and then hit a moving target 20 to 30 metres away within three to five seconds. If your first shot does not do the job, you will have less than five seconds to fire a second or third time. The entire event will be over in less then 20 seconds. I do not recommend that people rely on a rifle. Prevention of a conflict is your best option.

Foreign visitors, on tourist status in Canada, can bring a rifle or shot gun along for bear protection. You must however, declare it at the border. You are not allowed to bring pistols into Canada. When travelling with a guide, unless hunting is part of your trip itinerary, you do not need to worry about firearms. Generally, if I am not travelling in the heart of grizzly or polar bear country, I do not carry a weapon.

Permits are required to export any wildlife or wildlife parts from the Northwest Territories. People often forget that they must have a permit to take an old pair of caribou antlers out of the Territories. Many animals in the north, like the polar bear, are protected by the Convention on International Trade in Endangered Species of Fauna and Flora (C.I.T.E.S.). Polar bear hair for streamers can get you in a lot of trouble if you try to cross an international boundary. The Department of Renewable Resources, Government of the Northwest Territories can provide visitors with the latest information on wildlife in the area you plan to visit. For more information you can write to Conservation Education and Resource Development, Department of Renewable Resources, Government of the Northwest Territories, Box 600, 5102—50th Ave., Yellowknife, NWT, X1A 3S8.

Viewing archaeological sites is a major drawing card for many visitors. Fishermen should remember however, that the remains are fragile and can be easily destroyed by carelessly walking around on sites. It is illegal to remove artifacts or in any way to alter the remains of past human activity. More information on archaeological sites can be obtained by contacting the Senior Archaeologist, Prince of Wales Northern Heritage Centre, Department of Education, Culture and Employment, Government of the Northwest Territories, Box 1320, Yellowknife, NWT, X1A 2L9.

The Northwest Territories is the only jurisdiction in Canada where aboriginal people make up a majority of the population. Dene, Inuit and Inuvialuit are the original peoples. The Métis people who grew from intermarriage between the Dene and early Euro-Canadian settlers are an important part of that indigenous community.

Over the last 20 years, the Government of Canada and the Native people of the NWT, have been negotiating land claims to settle long standing grievances. The claims resulted from Canada's assumption of sovereignty over the land in the territories, without compensation to the original inhabitants who still hold "aboriginal" title.

If you are travelling on your own, you should be aware of the various land claim settlements. The following list of claim agencies can help you if you are in doubt. In most instances, however, a recreational wanderer travelling along a navigable waterway will not have any real problems.

The first claim was settled in 1984, when the Inuvialuit signed an agreement with the Government of Canada concerning traditional lands in the western Arctic. Casual recreational use on Inuvialuit lands is allowed as long as no significant damage or mischief occurs and/or Inuvialuit use and enjoyment of the land is not restricted. Those considering non-recreational or large group use of land within the Inuvialuit Settlement Region should contact the Inuvialuit Regional Corporation, Inuvik, NWT, XOE OTO.

The Gwich'in Comprehensive Land Claim Agreement of September 1991, for the lower Mackenzie Valley and the Sahtu Dene and Métis Comprehensive Land Claim Agreement of 1993, in the central Mackenzie Valley and on Great Bear Lake, both provide for the right of innocent passage along navigable waters. This allows non-claimants to fish and hunt water fowl along those flows. If you have any questions you can write to the Gwich'in Tribal Council, Inuvik, NWT, X0E 0T0; or the Sahtu Secretariat Inc., Deline, NWT, X0E 0H0.

According to the agreement between the Inuit of the Nunavut Settlement Area and Her Majesty the Queen in right of Canada, signed in 1993, access across Inuit owned lands is by consent only. The exception is the right of non-claimants to travel by water. This includes the recreational use of a 100-foot-wide strip of land bordering navigable rivers, lakes and the ocean. If you plan to travel in the eastern NWT through the Nunavut Claim Area, information can be obtained from Nunavut Tunngavik Inc., Suite 1510-130 Albert Street, Ottawa, Ontario or the Lands Department, Nunavut Tunngavik Inc. P.O. Box 1041, Cambridge Bay, NWT, X0E 0X0.

As of late 1995, there are still other land claims under negotiation in the western NWT—south of Great Bear Lake, around Great Slave Lake and in the upper Mackenzie River drainage. If you plan to travel on your own in these areas, the Aboriginal Rights Secretariat, Box 1320, Yellowknife, NWT, X1A 2L9 can provide you with relevant information relating to claims settled after this book has gone to press.

There is more to life than fishing. Each summer many of the communities hold music and arts festivals. They range from the Ikhalupik Jamboree in the tiny Inuvialuit community of Paulatuk, to the Midway Lake Festival near Fort McPherson and Folk on the Rocks in Yellowknife.

For the more competitive, there are a number of fishing derbies. Whale Cove, a small Inuit village on the west coast of Hudson's Bay sponsors a derby in late May to celebrate the end of winter. The community of Wha Ti holds a lake trout derby in August and Coppermine has one for Arctic charr in September. These events are a good opportunity to experience a northern community at a time when everyone is speaking the universal language of fish.

If your fishing trip is part of a plan to canoe a northern river, get accurate trip reports. I remember the time friends tried to pioneer a new route from Great Bear Lake to the Coppermine River. Their 50-mile upstream slog ended when they could not find a path through the boulders to make the 14-mile portage over the height-of-land to the Coppermine drainage. Fortunately, they were able to charter an aircraft from a fishing lodge to take them to the Coppermine River so that they could finish their trip. Other impromptu routes have left people in very dangerous circumstances. It is fun to scout new trips, but it takes a lot of advanced planning to make sure you are not going to end up stranded.

Having worked for the U.S. Forest Service in southeast Alaska, where we were required to be in constant radio contact with headquarters, it is refreshing to think about the remoteness of the Keele River with little to intrude on life. This freedom, however, has its price. If a party member is injured, it may be very difficult to get them to help.

In 1983, one of my crew accidentally injured his eye while poling a scows through a rapids on the Keele River. Atmospheric conditions blotted out radio transmissions on the first evening and so it was morning before we were able to raise anyone on the trappers' radiofrequency. The Wrigley Band Office promised to call the nurse in Fort Norman, but did not follow through before we lost radio contact. All that day, we carried him, blindfolded with gauze patches over his eyes, as the boats twisted their way through the rapids up the Keele River. Finally, on the evening of the second day, we raised Rosie Norwegian in Fort Norman. By that time it was 10 at night, and there was less than an hour and a half of flying time left before sunset.

The nurse in Fort Norman got a hold of bush pilot Martin Hartwell in his Cessna 185, over Great Bear Lake. Martin calculated he could reach our position within legal limits if he abandoned his current charter and headed immediately for the mountains. He told us to meet him on a straight stretch of the river about a mile and a half below our camp. We built a huge fire on a bar next to the river and waited. When we heard his plane, we set the blaze to act as a beacon in the gathering gloom. Martin circled once, and then landed. He taxied against a 12 knot current to the base of the rapids. We practically threw our crew member on board as Martin brought the plane around and started his run. We saw them lift off the river, as the Cessna disappeared into the shadow of the canyon walls. By the time Martin landed in Fort Norman, it was dark. The nurse put our friend on an air ambulance for Edmonton later the same night. Before morning, the surgeons had saved his eye. He was very fortunate.

Without a radio, you are on your own. Your safety when you are on your own depends on good planning, sound judgment, and luck. I firmly believe that luck is predicated by being properly prepared. That includes strong canoeing and wilderness skills, being in good cardiovascular shape,

having proper maps of the route in each canoe or boat, and checking difficult water before running it. If an accident does occur, it is important that everyone in the group understand rescue procedures and have first aid and CPR training. Unlike an urban setting, the first aider may have to stabilize the patient for a relatively long period of time. You must be prepared to deal with shock and hypothermia. The party should have a good first aid kit, and know where outfitters' camps and communities are located in case you need to head for help.

A lot of wilderness travellers scoff at the idea of including CPR as part of their preparations. All too often, people believe they could not keep a heart attack victim alive long enough to get help. While this maybe true, boating on cold northern waters may mean that you will need CPR to resuscitate a near drowned victim. Emersion in extremely cold water often allows people to be successfully revived who would be lost in warmer water. The U.S. Forest Service will not let anyone in the field on the Alaskan coast that does not have CPR. It has saved many lives.

The 1:1,000,000; 1:250,000 and 1:50,000 scale map sheets you will need to plan your trip are available from Tgit Geomatics Ltd., P.O. Box 244, Yellowknife, NWT, X1A 2N2 or 403-873-8438. I carry all three scales so that I am familiar with the country I fly over between our jumping off point and the trail head, as well as the river route. Parties have accidentally been dropped on the wrong lake. Can you imagine how frustrating it must have been to be set down miles from your intended destination. If the lake does not have an outlet, it can take a long time to flag down a passing float plane.

The river hygrographs that accompany canoe trip reports will give you an idea of the water levels you may encounter, but they are only a guide. When David Pelly did the river notes for our 1988 trip on the Kazan River, he based his description on his 1982 experience. Water levels in 1988, were nearly a metre higher. That drastically changed the character of the river. On mountain rivers, water levels can vary dramatically from one day to the next. An acquaintance who wishes to remain nameless to protect the guilty, told me the story of their trip on the Nahanni River. One morning, everyone woke up to discover that their packs had washed way. They had a horrible day chasing gear down the next six or seven miles of river. I bet they were glad they remembered to tie the canoes down before they went to bed.

I remember a night along the Mackenzie River at a Dene fish camp when even the experts got caught. When we landed, George Barnaby pitched our tent well above the flats where everyone else was camped. As he selected the site, George commented that he thought that the black clouds to the south might be a storm that would cause the river to rise. I got a great picture early the next morning of Wilfred Jackson running his boat through the front flap of the wall tent to load soggy sleeping bags.

For summer weather in the NWT, bring a parka and shorts. Even though daytime temperatures generally range between the high 30s and low 70s, it often freezes at night. Freeze hell, it

can snow. During the summer of 1984, when we worked at Fort Alexander on the Willow Lake River, the weather was great through the first two weeks of August. We were swimming every afternoon and generally having a wonderful time. One night a storm blew in and dropped eight inches of snow. The next morning George Boots went out with his snowmobile to haul wood in for the cabins. It took three days to melt.

In the wake of that storm, we were glad we had four season tents that shed the wind, and polar guard sleeping bags rated to 15 degrees F. Ever since my first polar guard sleeping bag got soaked on the Hayes River in northern Manitoba, I have been sold on poly filled sleeping bags for summer use in the north. My bag dried in a couple hours while my friend Jack Grieves' down bag remained damp for several days.

Given canoe trip restrictions on personal gear, preparing for a trip in the NWT, with its extreme variations in weather, is an art. I normally pack and repack my stuff sack a dozen times before I am happy with my choice of gear. Despite the need to compact gear as much as possible, I still prefer rubber rain gear to the new "high tech" stuff that is supposed to breathe. Once the wonder fabrics get dirty, they leak. Canoeing, I use my PFD (personal flotation device) as part of my thermal layering as well as emergency flotation, since I wear it whenever I am on the water. When I am travelling by boat, a floatation jacket with a thermal diaper is my standard jacket. My coat is large enough so that I can slip rain gear and sweaters and a wind breaker under it when they

Rangar Wesstrom and Doug Nelson cooking shore lunch on X Island, North Arm of Great Slave Lake.

are needed. There are good arguments to be made for both wool and synthetic piles as under garments in your layering scheme. I have both and pick and choose based on warmth versus bulk.

It is really easy to fill up your stuff sack. I always end up with my extra sweater pushed in with my sleeping bag. There is no better general footwear than slip-on rubber boots that come half way to your knee. They keep your feet dry getting in and out of the boats and on muskeg portages. I have a personal phobia about clothing that has loose nylon linings. If you dump and they get wet, nylon tends to cling to you when you try to take them off. I will never forget the image of a man from Oxford House, Manitoba being pulled out of Back Lake on the Hayes River. He had fallen out of his boat on a cold spring day. When he tried to take off his heavy parka so that he could swim back to the boat, his arms became entangled in the sleeves as the nylon lining clung to his shirt. Somehow during the struggle, his arms became pinned behind his back. When we pulled him out of the lake, it was obvious his efforts had been in vain. He had drowned.

When you are travelling on your own, you should file a Wilderness Trip Registration form with the RCMP at your point of departure. I would hate to have to stand the cost of a search and rescue, but it is better than dying because no one knew where you were or when you were due back.

What to do about bug dope? I carry a bug jacket. There is a choice between lose net weaves that are soaked each night in Deet based repellents and very fine weaves that simply keep the bugs out. The saturation jackets give you the power of Deet without having to put it directly on your skin. I use citronella based repellents when I need to apply something directly on my skin. Deet dissolves some plastics, removes paint, and damages graphite rods. When the plastic handle of my Swiss Army Knife turned to mush after touching it with a Deet soaked hand I got the message. On the other side of the argument, Deet is great for people who are extremely sensitive to bug bites and might be driven wild without it. I carry a small bag of baking powder and some Vitamin E cream in case one of us develops a bad case of bug bite itch. Buzzing, do you hear bugs buzzing, I guess one simply has to learn how to tune them out. Perhaps I am a wimp, but give me the mosquitoes and black flies of the NWT over the poisonous snakes and spiders that infest other regions of the world.

Having the appropriate skills for the trip you plan is very important. If you are not a wilderness traveller, there are a lot of guided trips and lodges that will look after everything for you. A trip to the Territories will be expensive. It is worth the time to plan an experience that fits your desires and budget. Being prepared for a variety of conditions will help insure the quality of your experience. A cold day on the water is a cold day on the water whether or not you have a guide in the boat. Who wants chattering teeth when after hours of experimentation, you have finally found the right streamer for a picky run of Arctic charr.

Please remember that though the north looks like a big empty place, it is also very fragile. Careless scars on the land take years to heal. Travel lightly, leaving as few traces of your passage as possible. Have a good trip

Mike Whittier with an Archtic charr at Wager Bay, near Hudson's Bay.

Photo by David Pelly

Giant Stonefly

Light Stonefly
Nymph

Dark Stonefly
Nymph

White Multicolor
Muddler

Yellow Multicolor
Muddler

Multicolor Muddler

Partridge and
Peacock

Partridge and
Orange

Royal Wulff

Gray Wulff

Parachute
Adams

Blue and Olive

Humpy

Goddard Caddis

(Peacock) Skating
Caddis

(Tan) Skating
Caddis

Bivisible

(Tan) Nelson's
Caddis

Dark Brown
Nelson's Caddis

Flies of the Northwest Territories

All flies except Bear Lake Herring and Stickleback Light tied by Gary Almeida

Megadiver

Brass Headed Wooly
Bugger

Red and Yellow Sea
Dance

Olive Wolly Bugger

Stickleback (light)

Whitlock's Matuka
Sculpin

Bear Lake Herring

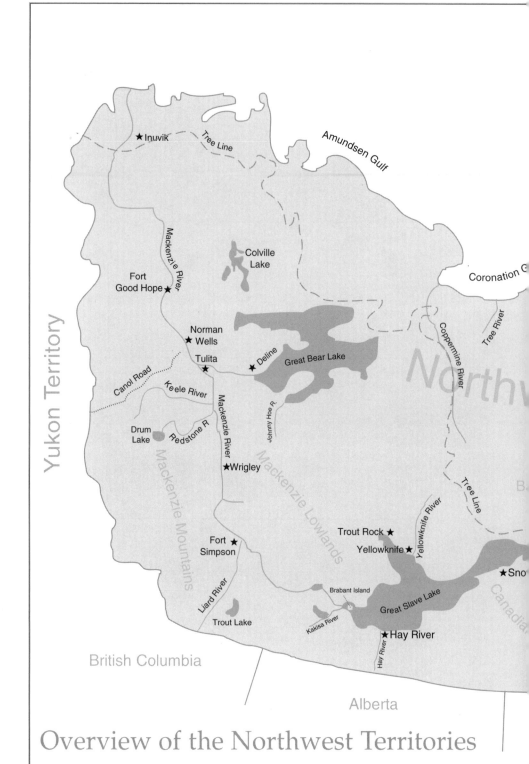

Overview of the Northwest Territories

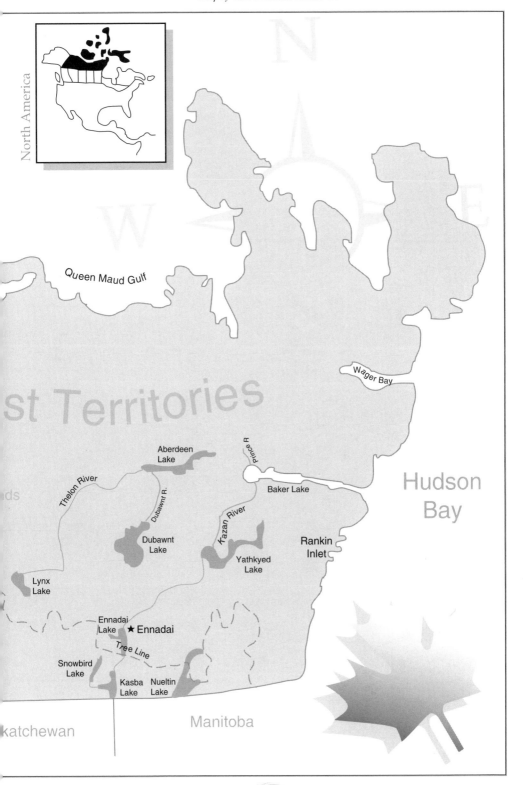

North America

Queen Maud Gulf

Wager Bay

st Territories

Aberdeen Lake

Prince R.

Baker Lake

Thelon River

Dubawnt R.

Kazan River

Hudson Bay

ds

Dubawnt Lake

Yathkyed Lake

Rankin Inlet

Lynx Lake

Ennadai Lake ★ Ennadai

Tree Line

Snowbird Lake

Kasba Lake

Nueltin Lake

Manitoba

katchewan